Messi and Ronaldo: Built for Greatness – A Kids Guide to Soccer Goats

The Secrets Behind How They Conquered The Soccer World

Max Reed

© Copyright 2025 - All rights reserved.

The content contained within this book may not be reproduced, duplicated or transmitted without direct written permission from the author or the publisher.

Under no circumstances will any blame or legal responsibility be held against the publisher, or author, for any damages, reparation, or monetary loss due to the information contained within this book, either directly or indirectly.

Legal Notice:

This book is copyright protected. It is only for personal use. You cannot amend, distribute, sell, use, quote or paraphrase any part, or the content within this book, without the consent of the author or publisher.

Disclaimer Notice:

Please note the information contained within this document is for educational and entertainment purposes only. All effort has been executed to present accurate, up to date, reliable, complete information. No warranties of any kind are declared or implied. Readers acknowledge that the author is not engaged in the rendering of legal, financial, medical or professional advice. The content within this book has been derived from various sources. Please consult a licensed professional before attempting any techniques outlined in this book.

By reading this document, the reader agrees that under no circumstances is the author responsible for any losses, direct or indirect, that are incurred as a result of the use of the information contained within this document, including, but not limited to, errors, omissions, or inaccuracies.

Table of Contents

INTRODUCTION 1

CHAPTER 1: THE EARLY DAYS 3

CHAPTER 2: THE ROAD TO STARDOM 13

CHAPTER 3: THE COMPETITIVE EDGE 23

CHAPTER 4: PINNACLES OF ACHIEVEMENT.................................33

CHAPTER 5: BEYOND THE FIELD 41

CHAPTER 6: THE PERSONAL SIDE OF GREATNESS 51

CHAPTER 7: THE ART OF MASTERY 59

CHAPTER 8: TEAMWORK AND LEADERSHIP 69

CHAPTER 9: CHALLENGES AND TRIUMPHS 79

CHAPTER 10: BONUS SECTION (FACTS AND TRIVIA): 87

CONCLUSION 111

REFERENCES 113

Introduction

Have you ever wondered what it takes to be the best of the best? To rise above the rest and leave your mark on the world? Well, let me tell you, it's not just about having talent or luck. It's about something much deeper, something that comes from within.

And that's exactly what we're going to explore in this book, "Messi and Ronaldo: Built for Greatness - A Kids Guide to Soccer Goats." We're going to dive into the lives of two of the greatest soccer players of all time and uncover the secrets behind their success.

Now, I know what you might be thinking. "But I'm just a kid! How can I relate to these superstars?" Trust me, I get it. But here's the thing: Messi and Ronaldo weren't always the legends they are today. They started out just like you and me - as kids with big dreams and a love for the game.

And that's what this book is all about. It's not just a boring old biography or a bunch of stats and figures. No way! We're going to have some fun along the way. We'll explore their lives, their triumphs, and their challenges, all while learning valuable lessons that we can apply to our own lives.

Whether you're a young athlete looking for inspiration, or an avid soccer fan, . It's packed with stories, trivia, and even some interactive challenges that will help you develop your own mental toughness and resilience. Because let's face it, life isn't always easy. We all face obstacles and setbacks. But it's how we respond to those challenges that defines us.

So, are you ready to join me on this journey? Are you ready to discover what it takes to be a champion, both on and off the field? Then let's get started!

Throughout this book, we'll alternate between the stories of Messi and Ronaldo, exploring the key moments and decisions that shaped their careers. We'll learn about their training routines, their mindset, and the values that have guided them to the top of their game.

But this isn't just about soccer. It's about life. It's about setting goals, working hard, and never giving up on your dreams. It's about being a good teammate, a good friend, and a good person.

So whether you're a die-hard soccer fan or just looking for some inspiration, this book has something for you. Get ready to laugh, to learn, and to be amazed by the incredible journeys of these two soccer legends.

Are you ready to discover the secrets of greatness? Then let's dive in and see what Messi and Ronaldo can teach us about reaching for the stars and never settling for second best.

Together, we'll learn that greatness isn't just about what you achieve, but about who you become along the way. So let's get started on this exciting adventure and see where it takes us!

Chapter 1:

The Early Days

You know, it's funny how the smallest places can give birth to the biggest dreams. Take Rosario, Argentina, and Madeira, Portugal, for example. They may not be the biggest or most famous places on Earth, but they sure know how to nurture greatness. You see, these places are where Lionel Messi and Cristiano Ronaldo first learned to kick a soccer ball. And boy, did they kick it far—so far that the whole world noticed.

1.1 Humble Beginnings in Rosario and Madeira

Let's start with Rosario. It's a city that lives and breathes soccer. Imagine a place where every street corner has kids playing soccer, each one dreaming of becoming the next big star. That's Rosario for you. It's not just a city; it's where Messi's journey began. The people there have a special love for Newell's Old Boys, a local club. It's where Messi first showed the world he had something special, even as a tiny kid running circles around his friends. But life wasn't all rainbows and unicorns. Economic struggles hit Rosario hard. Families had to work extra hard to make ends meet. Messi's family was no different. They lived in a simple home, where dreams were big, but wallets were small. Yet, the love for soccer brought everyone together. Community games were a big deal. It was like a festival, with everyone cheering for the kids on the field, hoping one of them would make it big.

Now, let's hop over to Madeira, an island that's as beautiful as it is challenging. Picture this: rugged cliffs, lush greenery, and the ocean as far as the eye can see. It's a paradise, but life isn't easy there. Resources were scarce, and families often struggled to get by. That's where Ronaldo comes in. He grew up in a humble home, where soccer was the escape from daily struggles. Ronaldo didn't have fancy fields or expensive gear. Nope. He had the streets and a ball. And that was enough. He played with friends, family, or even by himself, using every opportunity to hone his skills. The community was tight-knit. Everyone knew each other, and they all gathered to watch Ronaldo and his friends play. It was a time when soccer was more than just a game; it was a lifeline, a way to forget about the hardships and focus on the good stuff.

Messi and Ronaldo's early days were filled with signs of what was to come. In Rosario, Messi's talent was clear from the get-go. He played for Club Abanderado Grandoli and Newell's Old Boys, scoring goals that made people stop and stare. His small size didn't matter because his skill and passion were enormous. In Madeira, Ronaldo was the kid who wouldn't stop. He played with a fiery intensity that left others in awe. Street soccer was his training ground, where he learned to dribble, pass, and shoot with precision.

So there you have it. Two places, two kids, and a whole lot of dreams. Rosario and Madeira might be worlds apart, but they share a love for soccer that helped shape two of the greatest players the world has ever seen. It's amazing what a little love, a lot of passion, and a soccer ball can do. And who knows? Maybe the next big star is out there right now, kicking a ball on some street, dreaming of greatness.

1.2 The First Touch: Discovering Soccer Magic

Picture this: a young Lionel Messi, barely taller than the soccer ball itself, standing on a bumpy field in Rosario, Argentina. The sun shines bright, and the air buzzes with the cheers of friends and family. It's a moment that seems so simple yet holds the beginning of something extraordinary. That first kick, the ball rolling off his tiny foot, felt like magic. It was as if the ball knew it had found its partner. The joy on his face was pure and infectious. Everyone around could see it. In that heartbeat, Messi wasn't just playing; he was beginning to dream. That magical moment was more than just a kick. It was the spark that lit a fire inside him—a fire that said, "This is where I belong."

Across the ocean, in a world that felt both similar and different, a young Cristiano Ronaldo faced his own soccer awakening. In the backyard of his home in Madeira, Portugal, he honed his skills. The ground might have been uneven, and the ball might have been worn, but those things didn't matter. Ronaldo's determination made every kick count. Every practice session was a chance to get better. He played with a kind of focus that left no doubt about his goal. Despite the challenges, his confidence never wavered. Each moment with the ball was a step closer to his dreams. For Ronaldo, soccer was more than a game. It was a chance to prove himself.

Both Messi and Ronaldo found encouragement from those who saw their potential. In Rosario, local coaches noticed Messi's talent right away. They saw something special in how he moved with the ball. Their support and guidance helped him grow. In Madeira, Ronaldo's family played a huge role. They believed in him from the very start. Their faith in his abilities fueled his determination. They cheered him on, knowing he had something extraordinary. These early believers helped shape their paths, providing the encouragement needed to take risks and aim high.

Their early experiences highlight the contrast between structured and unstructured play. Messi found his rhythm in organized clubs, where practice routines and team strategies shaped his skills. He learned discipline and teamwork, understanding how each player contributes to the bigger picture. Ronaldo, on the other hand, embraced the freedom of street soccer. Without the constraints of formal training, he developed creativity and adaptability. He learned to think on his feet, using every inch of space to his advantage. This blend of structure and spontaneity helped them become the players they are today.

If you ever thought that first touches don't matter much, think again. That first kick, that first practice, those first moments of pure joy and determination, they all set the stage for greatness. These moments capture the magic that soccer holds—the magic that can turn a simple game into a lifelong passion. And just like Messi and Ronaldo, every young player has that magic waiting to be discovered.

1.3 Family Support: The Backbone of Success

When you think of superstars like Messi and Ronaldo, you might picture them sprinting across a field, leaving defenders in their dust. But behind those incredible moments are families who sacrificed everything to help them shine. Let's talk about Messi's grandmother. She was his biggest fan and a driving force in his early life. Imagine a little boy, wide-eyed and eager, being taken by his grandma to every game he could play. She stood on the sidelines, cheering louder than anyone else. Her belief in his talent was unshakable. She made sure he had the chance to show what he could do, no matter the obstacles. Her love and support fueled his confidence. And even today, Messi often credits her for being the first to recognize his potential.

Now, let's shift to Ronaldo's story. His mom, Maria Dolores, played a huge role in shaping his future. Life wasn't easy in Madeira. Maria worked long hours, but she always found time for Ronaldo. She did everything possible to ensure he had what he needed. She knew he had something special. Her sacrifices were many, but she made them gladly. Her dedication showed Ronaldo that hard work and commitment were key to success. She taught him that family stands by you, no matter what.

Both families faced challenges. Messi's family had to make a life-changing decision. Moving from Rosario to Barcelona was not simple. They left behind friends and family, all for the chance to give Messi a shot at greatness. It was a huge leap of faith, but they did it. They believed in him. The move meant leaving their comfort zone, starting fresh in a new country. It wasn't easy, but they knew it was necessary. Ronaldo's family had their share of struggles too. Money was tight, and there were times when making ends meet was a challenge. But they did whatever it took to support his training. Sometimes, that meant skipping personal comforts. But they knew they were investing in his future, and that made it worth it.

Through all these challenges, both families taught valuable lessons in resilience and teamwork. They showed that when you stick together, you can overcome anything. They were united in their support, facing tough times with courage. Messi learned the importance of family values from an early age. He saw firsthand how love and support could lift you up. Ronaldo's family taught him to never give up, to keep pushing forward even when the odds seemed against you. These lessons stayed with them, shaping their attitudes and mindset. They understood the power of unity and the strength that comes from having a strong support system.

Family isn't just about blood ties. It's about being there for each other, cheering each other on. Messi and Ronaldo both knew they could count on their families, no matter what. This foundation gave them the confidence to dream big and work hard. It reminded them that they weren't alone in their quests for greatness. They had their families behind them, every step of the way. This unwavering support became their driving force. It was the backbone of their success, pushing them to achieve what seemed impossible.

1.4 Overcoming Childhood Challenges

Imagine being told that you might never grow tall enough to play the sport you love. That was the reality for young Messi, who faced a growth hormone deficiency. This condition meant that he had to undergo regular medical treatments. It was a tough pill to swallow for someone who just wanted to play soccer like any other kid. Each injection was a reminder of the challenge he had to overcome. But instead of letting it defeat him, Messi faced it head-on. His size might have been small, but his heart was anything but. This battle wasn't just physical; it chipped away at his self-confidence too. He felt different from his peers, and not always in a good way. It was like having a shadow that followed him everywhere. Yet, Messi didn't let it overshadow his dreams. He tackled it with quiet strength, each step forward a victory in itself.

On the other hand, Ronaldo's hurdles were more about money, or rather, the lack of it. Growing up in Madeira, his family faced financial hardships that could have easily derailed his dreams. But instead of seeing limitations, Ronaldo saw opportunities. He knew that soccer was his ticket to a better life. That drive fueled his ambition, pushing him to practice harder than anyone else. Money was tight, but his spirit was unbreakable. He played with a fire in his belly, determined to rise above his circumstances. Every kick was a step toward a brighter future. He used adversity as fuel, turning challenges into stepping stones.

Messi and Ronaldo had to learn how to cope with their challenges early on. For Messi, medical treatments became part of his routine. It wasn't easy, but he understood that it was necessary. Alongside his treatments, he immersed himself in training. The field was his sanctuary, a place where he could forget about his struggles and just be a kid chasing a ball. Support from his family and coaches was crucial. They believed in him, giving him the strength to keep going. For Ronaldo, relentless practice was his way of coping. The hardships he faced only made him work harder. He spent hours honing his skills, often practicing until the sun set. His family stood by him, offering encouragement and support. They believed in his talent, knowing it was his best chance to change their lives.

Through these challenges, Messi and Ronaldo developed character traits that would define them. Messi learned humility and perseverance. Despite his struggles, he remained grounded, never letting his condition define him. He kept pushing forward, proving that determination could overcome any obstacle. His perseverance became his superpower, enabling him to achieve greatness. Ronaldo, on the other hand, embodied resilience and determination. He refused to let financial hardships dictate his future. Instead, he used them as motivation to excel. His resilience was unyielding, driving him to achieve what seemed impossible. His determination became his trademark, a testament to his unwavering spirit.

These early challenges shaped Messi and Ronaldo in ways that went beyond the soccer field. They taught them the value of hard work and the importance of never giving up. They learned that obstacles were merely opportunities in disguise. Their stories remind us that while the path to greatness isn't always easy, the lessons learned along the way are priceless. As young athletes, it's important to remember that everyone faces challenges. It's how we respond that truly matters. Just like Messi and Ronaldo, you have the power to turn your challenges into triumphs. So, lace up your boots, face your obstacles head-on, and remember that greatness is within your reach.

1.5 Early Inspirations: Role Models and Heroes

Growing up, we all have that one person we look up to. For Messi and Ronaldo, these figures weren't just people on TV. They were legends who seemed to defy gravity and reality with every move they made on the soccer field. In Rosario, Messi's eyes would light up whenever he watched Diego Maradona. The way Maradona danced with the ball was like watching magic unfold. He wasn't just a player; he was an artist, painting beautiful pictures on the field with his feet. Messi would watch old tapes of Maradona's games, studying each dribble, each feint, with the kind of focus that only true admiration can inspire. He saw in Maradona a reflection of what he could become—a maestro with the ball, a leader on the pitch. This was no small influence. It was a spark that ignited a fire deep within Messi, guiding him as he honed his skills and developed his own style of play.

Meanwhile, in Madeira, Ronaldo found his inspiration in Eusébio, another soccer giant whose legacy left a lasting mark on the sport. Eusébio's power and grace were something young Ronaldo admired deeply. Watching him play was like watching a lion in action—strong, fearless, and elegant. Ronaldo was captivated by Eusébio's ability to score goals from anywhere on the pitch. He wanted to be just like him. So, he practiced tirelessly, mimicking Eusébio's techniques, trying to capture that same magic in his own game. Ronaldo's admiration for Eusébio was more than just a fan's adoration. It was a driving force, pushing him to dream bigger, to work harder, and to never settle for anything less than being the best.

These role models played a crucial role in shaping Messi and Ronaldo's aspirations. They weren't just players; they were beacons of what could be achieved. Messi's emulation of Maradona wasn't about copying every move. It was about understanding the passion and creativity that Maradona brought to the game. Messi learned to see soccer as an art form, where his unique vision and skill could shine. Ronaldo, on the other hand, took Eusébio's physical style and made it his own. He combined strength with speed, creating a style that was both powerful and precise. Each of their idols taught them important lessons, not just about soccer, but about carrying themselves with dignity and pride.

The impact of these heroes reached beyond the field. They inspired values that Messi and Ronaldo would carry throughout their careers. Watching Maradona taught Messi the importance of humility, even when you're on top of the world. He learned that true greatness isn't about being the loudest or the flashiest, but about letting your actions speak for themselves. Ronaldo, inspired by Eusébio, understood the value of hard work and resilience. Eusébio had faced many challenges in his career, and Ronaldo saw how perseverance and dedication could overcome any obstacle. These lessons were as valuable as any training session, helping to shape the men they would become.

Having these role models gave Messi and Ronaldo motivation to reach higher and push further. It wasn't just about winning trophies or scoring goals. It was about becoming the best versions of themselves. Their idols showed them that it was possible to rise from anywhere and achieve anything with enough determination. They learned that the path to greatness is paved with hard work, integrity, and a little bit of magic.

As we wrap up these early chapters of their lives, it's clear that the seeds of greatness were planted early on. The influence of their heroes, combined with their own unique talents, set Messi and Ronaldo on a path toward soccer immortality. They remind us that no matter where we start, with the right inspiration and a lot of heart, we can achieve incredible things. So, ask yourself—who inspires you? What dreams are you ready to chase? Remember, the sky's the limit.

Chapter 2:

The Road to Stardom

Alright, let's dive into the next chapter of Messi and Ronaldo's lives. Imagine a place where dreams aren't just dreams, but plans in action. That's what youth academies are all about. Think of them as the Hogwarts of soccer, minus the magic wands and Quidditch, of course. These academies are where soccer dreams take root and grow into something spectacular. For Messi and Ronaldo, these were places where their potential was nurtured and honed.

Messi found his second home at La Masia, FC Barcelona's famous youth academy. Picture a grand old farmhouse, buzzing with young talent. That's La Masia. Here, Messi wasn't just a kid from Argentina; he became part of a legacy. La Masia is known for shaping world-class players, and Messi was one of its brightest stars. The academy didn't just teach him how to play soccer; it taught him the philosophy of the game. It was all about technical skills, creativity, and playing with heart. Messi learned to weave magic on the field, a skill that would set him apart in the years to come.

Meanwhile, over in Portugal, Ronaldo was making waves at the Sporting CP Academy. This place is legendary for producing top-notch players, and Ronaldo was no exception. Here, he was more than just a kid with a big dream. He was a force of nature. The academy focused on developing not just skills, but also discipline and mental strength. Ronaldo's time at Sporting CP was all about pushing limits and reaching new heights. It was the perfect playground for someone with his ambition and energy.

Getting into these academies wasn't a walk in the park. Oh no, it was like trying to find a shiny Pokémon—rare and requires a lot of effort. The selection process was tough. These kids had to go through trials and evaluations that tested every aspect of their game. It was intense. But Messi and Ronaldo stood out. They had something special, something that made coaches stop and take notice. In these academies, competition was fierce. Every player wanted to prove they were the best. But it was this environment that pushed Messi and Ronaldo to become better, to strive for excellence.

The support systems in these academies were nothing short of amazing. Coaches weren't just there to teach soccer; they were mentors, guiding these young players through the ups and downs of their journey. Messi had mentors who helped him refine his skills, teaching him the importance of teamwork and strategy. Ronaldo, on the other hand, had coaches who taught him the value of hard work and resilience. These mentors played a crucial role in shaping their careers, offering advice and encouragement when it was needed most.

Balancing education and training was another challenge. For Messi, living in Barcelona meant adapting to a new culture and language. But he was a quick learner, both on and off the field. He balanced school with soccer, making sure he was growing as a person, not just a player. Ronaldo also had to juggle academics with his training. He knew that education was important, and he made sure to stay on top of his studies while pursuing his dream. Their determination to excel in all areas set them apart, showing that being a great athlete also means being a well-rounded individual.

Exercise Time: Reflecting on Your Own Academy Dreams

Think about your own goals. What do you want to achieve? Write down three things you can do this week to get closer to your dreams. It could be practicing a new skill, learning something new, or just spending time with family. Remember, every small step counts. Just like Messi and Ronaldo, you have the power to turn your dreams into reality.

Training Like a Pro: Discipline and Routine

Life in a soccer academy isn't just about kicking a ball around. It's a world of routines and discipline. Imagine waking up before the sun even thinks of rising. That's what Messi and Ronaldo did every morning. They started their days with early training sessions, setting the tone for their futures. This wasn't just about practicing shots or dribbling around cones. It was about building a foundation of discipline that would carry them through their entire careers.

Physical conditioning played a huge role in their routines. You see, being a top athlete isn't just about skill. It's about being in peak physical shape. Messi had to focus on his agility and speed, using drills that tested his limits. Ronaldo, on the other hand, was all about strength and endurance. He was a regular at the gym, pushing himself to lift heavier or run faster. These training sessions weren't just about getting fit. They were about testing their limits and pushing beyond them.

Discipline was the name of the game. Sticking to a strict schedule was key. It meant sacrificing a lot of things that other kids might take for granted. Like staying up late or hanging out with friends. Both Messi and Ronaldo knew that to be the best, they had to make tough choices. They had to prioritize training above all else. This dedication taught them the value of consistency. They learned that showing up every day and putting in the work, even when they didn't feel like it, was what made the difference.

These routines shaped more than just their bodies. They shaped their minds. Developing a strong mental fortitude was just as important as building muscles. Messi learned to focus on his goals, blocking out distractions. Ronaldo developed a mindset of resilience, always aiming to outperform himself. Their structured training laid the groundwork for their professional longevity. It taught them how to handle pressure and stay cool in high-stakes situations.

Messi's commitment was evident in his early morning practices. While most kids his age were still dreaming, he was out on the field, perfecting his craft. He practiced his dribbles and shots, working on his precision. Ronaldo was no different. He spent countless hours in the gym, even after a full day of training. He pushed himself to the limit, determined to be stronger and faster. This level of dedication wasn't easy. But it was necessary.

Their commitment didn't go unnoticed. Coaches and teammates saw their drive and determination. It inspired those around them to work harder too. Messi and Ronaldo set the standard for what it meant to be a professional athlete. They showed that success wasn't just about talent. It was about putting in the hard work day in and day out.

These routines and discipline became second nature to them. They weren't just habits; they were a way of life. Messi and Ronaldo embraced the grind. They knew every drop of sweat, every aching muscle, was a step towards greatness. They didn't just train their bodies; they trained their minds and spirits. Their routines taught them the value of perseverance. They learned that the path to success was paved with sweat and sacrifice.

Now, think about your own life. What routines can you put in place to achieve your goals? Maybe it's waking up a little earlier to practice a skill. Or maybe it's setting aside time each day to work on something you're passionate about. Whatever it is, remember that discipline and routine are your allies. They're the building blocks to achieving your dreams, just like they were for Messi and Ronaldo.

Facing Rejection: The Path to Perseverance

Imagine being told you're too small to play the sport you love. That's exactly what happened to Messi. Coaches looked at him and saw a kid who might not grow tall enough to compete at the highest level. It was tough. When you're young and dreaming big, hearing that you're not enough can sting. But for Messi, those words didn't stop him. They fueled him. He was determined to show everyone that size didn't define talent. With every dribble and pass, he set out to prove them wrong. He turned doubt into determination, using it as motivation to push harder and play smarter.

Now, picture Ronaldo, a young boy full of energy and ambition. He had his own set of challenges. Critics said he was too flashy, all style and no substance. They doubted his ability to play in bigger leagues. It was a lot for anyone to handle, especially when all you want to do is prove yourself. But Ronaldo didn't let the negativity bring him down. Instead, he took every criticism as a challenge. He wanted to show that he wasn't just about tricks and flair. He was about goals, teamwork, and winning. His response to doubt was simple: work harder than anyone else.

Facing rejection and criticism is never easy. It can mess with your head. You might start questioning yourself, wondering if you're good enough. Messi and Ronaldo both felt that. They had moments of doubt. But they also had something else—support. Their families and mentors stood by them, offering encouragement and belief. They reminded Messi that his talent was undeniable, and they told Ronaldo that his flair was part of what made him special. This support was like a safety net, catching them when they felt like falling. It gave them the strength to keep going when the going got tough.

Perseverance became their secret weapon. Messi knew he couldn't change his height, but he could perfect his skills. He could outplay and outthink his opponents. So, he focused on his technique, turning every practice into an opportunity to grow. Ronaldo, on the other hand, embraced his critics. He worked tirelessly to improve every aspect of his game. He wanted to be more than just a showman; he wanted to be a leader. Their perseverance paid off. They kept pushing through, no matter how many times they stumbled. They learned that every setback was a setup for a comeback.

These experiences taught them invaluable lessons. Resilience became their armor, protecting them from the harshness of the outside world. They learned that adversity wasn't a roadblock; it was a stepping stone. It was a chance to prove their mettle, to show the world what they were made of. They grew stronger, not just as players, but as individuals. They realized that challenges weren't there to stop them. They were there to make them stronger, smarter, and more determined.

Messi and Ronaldo's stories remind us that rejection isn't the end. It's often the beginning of something great. It's a chance to dig deep, find your strength, and rise above the noise. So, whether you're facing criticism on the field or in life, remember that you're not alone. Everyone faces setbacks. It's how you respond that counts. Keep pushing, keep fighting, and never let anyone tell you that you can't achieve your dreams. Because just like Messi and Ronaldo, you have the power to turn the impossible into the possible. Keep your head up, and keep moving forward.

First Breaks: Seizing Opportunities

Imagine being a teenager and suddenly finding yourself standing on a field, wearing the iconic jersey of FC Barcelona. That was

Messi's reality when he made his debut with the senior team. It was a match against Espanyol, and the world held its breath. Here was this young kid, small in stature but huge in talent, about to show everyone what he could do. The pressure was immense, but Messi didn't let it faze him. He played with the natural ease and confidence that had become his signature style. His first touch on the ball was electric, and the crowd could sense something special. This was the moment when Messi truly stepped into the spotlight. Everyone could see that he wasn't just another player; he was a force of nature.

Meanwhile, over in Portugal, a young Ronaldo was making waves at Sporting CP. His standout performance came during a match against Moreirense, where he scored two goals and left everyone in awe. This wasn't just luck. It was the culmination of years of hard work and dedication. Ronaldo seized this opportunity with both hands, making it clear that he was destined for greatness. His speed, agility, and flair on the field captured the attention of fans and scouts alike. It was a performance that screamed, "Notice me!" And notice they did. Ronaldo's talent was undeniable, and it wasn't long before the world took note.

The circumstances that led to these breakthrough moments were a mix of talent and timing. For Messi, it was the faith of his coach, Frank Rijkaard, who saw potential beyond his size. Rijkaard gave Messi the chance to shine, and Messi didn't disappoint. He made an immediate impact, dazzling teammates and opponents alike. This was his moment to prove that he belonged on the world stage. For Ronaldo, it was the keen eye of Sir Alex Ferguson, the legendary manager of Manchester United. Ferguson saw something extraordinary in Ronaldo. He saw a player who could change the game with his presence. This recognition led to Ronaldo's transfer to Manchester United, a move that would shape his career in ways he couldn't have imagined.

Timing and preparation played crucial roles in these pivotal moments. Both Messi and Ronaldo were ready when opportunity knocked. They had put in the hours, honed their skills, and were prepared to seize their chance. It wasn't just about being in the right place at the right time. It was about being ready to show the world what they could do. Their talent and hard work fused together, creating a perfect storm of brilliance. Messi's debut wasn't just another game, and Ronaldo's performance wasn't just another match. These were the moments that defined their careers and set them on the path to becoming legends.

Messi's immediate impact on the team was undeniable. He brought a new energy, a new style of play that was both mesmerizing and effective. His ability to control the ball and create opportunities was unmatched. He became the heartbeat of the team, influencing every game he played. Ronaldo's move to Manchester United was a turning point. He embraced the challenge of playing in a more competitive league. He worked tirelessly to adapt and improve, becoming one of the most feared players in the Premier League. His time at United helped him develop into a more complete player, one who could dominate any game.

These first breaks were more than just moments in time. They were the catalysts that propelled Messi and Ronaldo into the professional spotlight. They showed the world that these two young players weren't just talented; they were exceptional. Their stories remind us that when preparation meets opportunity, incredible things can happen. It's about being ready to step up when the moment arrives, about turning potential into reality.

Rising Stars: Making a Mark on the Field

Once Messi started playing for Barcelona's first team, he wasn't just another player on the pitch. He was a game-changer. His ability to see the game differently, almost like he had a sixth sense, meant he could carve paths through defenses that others couldn't even dream of. His vision was something else. He'd spot a teammate in the perfect spot before anyone else knew they were even there. His passes weren't just accurate; they were magical. They had a way of bending reality, of finding the impossible opening. This creativity added a new flair to Barcelona's play style. The team became known for its fluid, fast-paced play, a style that was as beautiful to watch as it was effective. Messi wasn't just adapting to Barcelona's style; he was shaping it. He made everyone around him better, lifting the entire team to new heights.

Ronaldo, over in England, was making waves at Manchester United. He brought something fresh and electrifying to the team. His speed was almost unthinkable. Ronaldo could outrun almost anyone. But it wasn't just about speed. He had power, an ability to score from almost anywhere. Give him a sliver of space, and he'd find the net. He was the epitome of a goal machine. His ability to rise for headers, his skill in taking free kicks, and his knack for being in the right place at the right time—all these traits made him a formidable force. Ronaldo's presence on the field meant United always had a shot at victory. His contributions led to countless wins and trophies. He turned tight matches in their favor, delivering when it mattered most.

But their path wasn't all sunshine and rainbows. Transitioning to professional play was tough. They had to face a level of competition that was faster, more strategic, and more intense than anything they'd known before. Messi had to adjust to being marked by defenders twice his size and strength. He had to figure out how to use his agility to his advantage, to dance around his opponents like he was choreographing a ballet. Ronaldo had to learn to channel his flair into something that contributed to the team's success. It wasn't just about dazzling the crowd; it was about winning matches. Both players had to grow not just as individual stars, but as leaders who could inspire their teammates and drive team success.

What set them apart was their ability to adapt and excel in these challenging environments. Messi's vision and creativity were unparalleled. He saw the game as a series of puzzles, and he always seemed to have the right pieces. He could turn a simple pass into a work of art. Ronaldo's athleticism was jaw-dropping. He was a powerhouse of a player, with the strength of a forward and the speed of a winger. His ability to score goals was second to none. Whether it was a powerful shot from distance or a delicate chip over the goalkeeper, Ronaldo had it all. These skills, combined with their relentless work ethic, made them standouts in the world of soccer.

As their skills shone on the field, so did their reputations off it. Both players began to collect accolades and awards that recognized their incredible talent. Messi started earning praise as the best young player in Spain, and Ronaldo began gathering trophies for his performances in England. The media couldn't get enough of them, and fans around the world began to follow their every move. People wanted to see what these two rising stars would do next. They were no longer just players; they were becoming icons, the faces of a new generation of soccer.

Their early professional careers marked the beginning of something extraordinary. They were setting the stage for their legendary status, building a legacy that would inspire millions. Their journey was only just beginning, but already they had proven they belonged among the best. Next, we'll explore how their influence continued to grow, shaping not just their teams but the entire world of soccer.

Chapter 3:

The Competitive Edge

You know that feeling when you trip in front of your whole class? It's embarrassing, right? But what's more important is how you get back up. That's mental resilience, and it's super important in sports. Messi and Ronaldo know this well. They've faced their own setbacks, but they didn't let that stop them. Instead, they used these moments to come back stronger. It's kind of like when you fail a level in a video game and just keep trying until you beat the boss.

Imagine Messi, tearing a hamstring and being sidelined for a whopping 59 days. That's like missing out on two months of soccer practice, school games, and everything in between. But did Messi sulk? Nope. He focused on his recovery, each day getting stronger. When he came back, he didn't just play; he scored twice in a single match. Talk about a comeback! It was as if he had never missed a day. He showed everyone that a setback is just a setup for a comeback. And that's a lesson in resilience right there.

Ronaldo, on the other hand, faced a different kind of challenge. Imagine being one of the best players in the world and getting benched. Ouch, right? It's like being chosen last for a team despite being the fastest runner. But Ronaldo didn't let it get him down. He took it as a challenge. When he got his chance again, he made it count. He scored in the penalty shootout, proving that he still had what it takes. His determination was clear: never give up, no matter what others say.

Both these legends use visualization techniques to keep their minds sharp. It's like imagining yourself scoring the winning goal or acing that math test. Visualization helps them stay focused and ready for the challenges ahead. They also have a strong support network. Coaches, family, and friends all cheer them on, reminding them of their strengths. Having people who believe in you can make a world of difference. It's like having your own personal cheer squad by your side.

Building resilience isn't just about bouncing back once. It's about developing a never-give-up attitude. Messi and Ronaldo have mastered this art. They've learned to adapt and evolve, no matter the obstacles. Their ability to keep going, even when things get tough, is what sets them apart. They show us that success doesn't happen overnight. It's a journey filled with ups and downs. But with resilience, you can face anything that comes your way.

So, next time you face a challenge, remember Messi and Ronaldo. Remember how they've turned setbacks into comebacks. And remember that you too have the power to bounce back. Whether it's a missed shot or a tough day at school, resilience can help you rise above. Keep pushing, keep striving, and never lose sight of your goals. Because just like these soccer greats, you too can achieve greatness.

Quick Exercise: Building Your Resilience Muscle

Grab a piece of paper and jot down a recent setback you faced. Maybe it was a tough game or a bad grade. Now, list three ways you can turn that setback into a comeback. Perhaps it's practicing more or seeking help from a friend. Keep this list handy. Next time you face a challenge, remind yourself of these strategies and push forward with confidence.

3.2 Handling Pressure: Staying Cool Under Fire

Imagine stepping onto a field with thousands of eyes on you, every single one expecting you to perform miracles. That's the kind of pressure Messi and Ronaldo deal with every game. It's not just about playing soccer; it's about handling the weight of the world on your shoulders. High-stakes matches, like the Champions League finals, bring a level of intensity that's hard to describe. Every pass, every shot, every move counts. The media waits to pounce on any mistake, and fans have sky-high expectations. Teammates rely on you to lead and inspire. It can feel overwhelming, like standing in the middle of a storm.

But Messi and Ronaldo have figured out how to stay calm in these intense moments. They have their own ways to keep cool under fire. Take breathing exercises, for instance. You might think it sounds simple, but it's super effective. Deep breaths help calm the nerves. They bring focus back to the game and away from the noise. Mindfulness practices, like staying present and not worrying about what might happen, are key. These techniques help them block out distractions and focus on the task at hand. It's like hitting the pause button on everything else and zoning in on what really matters.

Both players have their own pre-game rituals. These routines help them find their zone and get into the right mindset. For Messi, it might be listening to music or doing a specific warm-up. For Ronaldo, it could be visualizing the game and planning his moves. These rituals become a safe space, a way to mentally prepare and find calm before the storm. They aren't just habits; they're part of a mental toolkit that helps them face pressure head-on. By sticking to these routines, they create a sense of familiarity and control, even when everything around them feels chaotic.

Messi has proven time and again that he thrives under pressure. Just look at his Champions League performances. When the stakes are high, he often steps up with decisive goals that turn the tide. It's as if the pressure unlocks a hidden level of skill. Ronaldo is known for his iconic free-kicks in crucial moments. When his team needs a goal, he delivers with precision and confidence. These clutch performances show their ability to rise to the occasion. They remind us that pressure isn't just something to endure; it's something to use to your advantage.

Experience plays a huge role in how they handle pressure. They've been in high-pressure situations countless times, and each one teaches a lesson. They've learned what works and what doesn't. With every success, their confidence grows. They know they can handle whatever comes their way because they've done it before. This confidence isn't just about skill; it's about trust in themselves. It's about knowing that they have what it takes to succeed. Through repeated success, they've built a mental armor that shields them from doubt and fear.

Messi and Ronaldo show that handling pressure isn't about being fearless. It's about being prepared. It's about using every tool at your disposal to stay calm and focused. And when the moment comes, it's about seizing it with both hands, knowing that you have the strength and skill to come out on top. Pressure becomes an ally, pushing them to achieve greatness, even when the world is watching.

3.3 The Art of Focus: Staying on Target

Ever try to focus on homework with a noisy TV blaring in the background? It's tough, right? Well, imagine trying to play world-class soccer with thousands of fans shouting your name, cameras flashing, and a rival team doing everything they can to throw you off. That's the reality for Messi and Ronaldo. Focus isn't just a skill for them; it's their superpower. It allows them to perform at their peak, making sure they're always in the right place at the right time. Concentration during matches is crucial. Even the tiniest lapse can lead to a missed goal or a defensive slip. It's like playing a video game where one mistake can mean game over. They have to keep their minds sharp, ignoring the chaos around them. Off the field, distractions come in many forms. Social media, interviews, and even personal life can pull at their attention. But Messi and Ronaldo have learned to tune it all out, keeping their eyes on the prize.

Techniques for maintaining focus are as varied as the players themselves. Messi, for instance, is known for his ability to block out negative noise. It's like he has an internal mute button that he presses whenever things get too loud. He sets clear and achievable goals for each game, focusing on what he needs to do rather than what others expect of him. This helps him stay grounded and in control. Ronaldo takes a slightly different approach. He thrives on setting targets and smashing them, always pushing himself to do better. His goals aren't just about scoring; they're about improving every aspect of his play. This disciplined approach helps him stay focused, even when the pressure is on.

Focus leads to pivotal moments. We've all seen Messi weave through defenders like they're standing still. His dribbling precision is legendary, especially in tight spaces where one wrong move could mean losing the ball. It's almost like watching an artist paint his masterpiece, each touch of the ball carefully calculated. Ronaldo, on the other hand, is known for his ability to execute under defensive pressure. When surrounded by opponents, he doesn't panic. Instead, he finds the perfect moment to strike, often turning a challenging situation into a goal opportunity. These moments of brilliance aren't just luck; they're the result of intense focus and dedication.

Decision-making and performance consistency go hand in hand with focus. On the pitch, quick decisions can change the course of a game. Messi's ability to read the field and make split-second choices is unmatched. Whether it's passing to a teammate or taking a shot himself, his focus ensures he makes the right call. Ronaldo's consistency is a testament to his focus. Game after game, he delivers top-level performances, never letting his guard down. This level of focus is what separates the good from the great. It's what makes Messi and Ronaldo not just players, but legends. Their ability to concentrate and stay on target means they're always ready to seize the moment, no matter the odds. It's a lesson in the power of focus, showing that with the right mindset, anything is possible.

3.4 Tactical Brilliance: Outthinking Opponents

Think of soccer like a giant chess game, but with a lot more running and excitement. It's all about being one step ahead, knowing what the other player might do before they even do it. This is called soccer intelligence, and Messi and Ronaldo have it in spades. They don't just play the game. They think the game. They read the field like a book, spotting patterns and predicting moves that leave others scratching their heads in wonder. It's like having a superpower. They know when to attack, when to pass, and when to hold back. This awareness lets them adapt their strategies as the game flows, shifting gears as needed. They aren't just playing; they're orchestrating the game like a conductor with an orchestra.

Messi's ability to find and exploit spaces is a thing of beauty. Imagine running through a maze where walls keep shifting. Messi always finds the open path. He dances through defenses, finding gaps no one else sees. He knows exactly where the ball needs to go and how to get it there. It's not just about speed. It's about timing and precision. Ronaldo has his own brand of brilliance. His strategic positioning is like that of an expert chess player. He finds himself in the right spot at the right time, ready to strike. He understands the field so well that he can almost predict where the ball will end up. His opponents often feel like they're a step behind, always chasing but never quite catching up. His knack for being where the action is makes him a constant threat.

Tactical brilliance shines brightest in action. Picture Messi, weaving through defenders, not just with his feet but with his mind. He orchestrates plays, setting up teammates with perfect passes. It's as if he has eyes in the back of his head. He creates opportunities out of thin air, turning impossible situations into clear chances. Ronaldo's off-the-ball movement is equally impressive. While everyone else is focused on the ball, Ronaldo is busy getting into position. He knows when to charge forward and when to hang back. This movement creates scoring chances even when he doesn't have the ball. He pulls defenders out of position, opening up spaces for his team to exploit.

Their tactical understanding adds another layer to their game. They're not just individual stars. They're leaders who elevate team dynamics and cohesion. Their vision helps teammates see the game differently. They inspire others to think creatively and strategically. Messi's vision helps him connect with his teammates on another level. They understand his intentions and respond accordingly. His ability to orchestrate plays makes him a natural leader on the field. Ronaldo's strategic positioning and movement set an example for his teammates. He shows them the value of anticipation and awareness. His presence alone changes how the team plays, elevating their performance. This leadership is what sets them apart as true legends. They're not just great players. They're great thinkers, always outsmarting their opponents, always one step ahead.

3.5 Self-Belief: The Power of Confidence

You know that feeling when you just know you're going to ace that test or score that winning goal? That's self-belief, and it's like having your personal cheerleader inside your head. For Messi and Ronaldo, self-belief isn't just a nice-to-have. It's crucial for achieving greatness. When times get tough, like when the score is tied and the clock is ticking down, they rely on their own confidence to push through. They trust their abilities, knowing they've put in the hours of practice. It's that inner voice saying, "You've got this," even when the pressure is on. Their confidence shines brightest during high-risk plays, those moments that can change the game. Whether it's Messi dribbling past defenders or Ronaldo taking a shot from long distance, their belief in themselves is their secret weapon.

So, how do they keep that confidence alive and kicking? It's not just about skills. It's also about how they carry themselves. Have you ever noticed how Messi and Ronaldo celebrate their goals? Those fist pumps and smiles aren't just for show. They boost their morale and send a message to everyone watching: "I'm here to win." Their body language is full of assurance. They stand tall, with a presence that commands respect. It's like they've got an invisible aura of confidence that makes everyone around them take notice. This self-assurance helps them stay steady, even when things don't go as planned. It's not arrogance; it's the quiet confidence that comes from knowing they've done the work.

There are moments in their careers when self-belief made all the difference. Picture Messi weaving through defenders with the ball glued to his feet. His solo goals are a testament to his individual brilliance. He trusts in his ability to make magic happen, even when the odds seem stacked against him. Ronaldo shines in high-pressure situations too. Think about those decisive penalties he's taken, with the whole world watching. It's just him, the ball, and the goal. His confidence in those moments is rock-solid, and it's what helps him deliver when it counts. Self-belief turns challenges into opportunities, allowing them to perform at their best when it matters most.

Their confidence doesn't just lift their own game; it inspires everyone around them. When Messi and Ronaldo step onto the field with their heads held high, they lead by example. Their unwavering self-belief shows teammates and fans that anything is possible. They inspire others to believe in their own potential, to dream big and chase those dreams relentlessly. It's a ripple effect. Their confidence spreads like wildfire, igniting a spark in everyone they meet. They remind us that with belief, we can overcome any obstacle and reach for the stars.

As this chapter wraps up, remember that self-belief is a powerful tool. It's about trusting yourself, even when you're not sure what lies ahead. Just like Messi and Ronaldo, you have the power to build your confidence and use it to achieve greatness. So, stand tall, believe in your abilities, and let your inner cheerleader guide you to success.

Chapter 4:

Pinnacles of Achievement

Ever tried juggling a soccer ball and lost count after three? Now, imagine if you could do it 91 times—while scoring goals in real games, not just in your backyard. That's what Lionel Messi did in 2012, setting a world record for the most goals scored in a single calendar year. Picture this: 79 goals for Barcelona and 12 for Argentina, leaving defenders scratching their heads, wondering how this tiny player kept finding the back of the net. Messi didn't just break the old record of 85 goals set by Gert Müller in 1972; he shattered it. It was like he was playing a video game on cheat mode, but it was all real. This kind of achievement shows why Messi is often called the GOAT—Greatest Of All Time.

On the other hand, Cristiano Ronaldo was busy rewriting the record books in the UEFA Champions League. This competition is like the World Cup of club soccer, and Ronaldo seemed to own it. He became the fastest player to reach 100 goals in the tournament, a feat that left fans gasping and opponents scrambling. It's like racing through your favorite video game and beating all the bosses in record time. Ronaldo's knack for scoring in crucial moments made him a legend. He holds the record for the most goals scored in the Champions League, with 140 goals to his name. It's as if scoring goals was as easy as breathing for him.

These records aren't just numbers on a sheet. They're milestones that changed soccer history. When Messi scored his 91st goal, he set a new standard for what was possible. Fans worldwide celebrated as if they'd scored the goals themselves. Ronaldo's Champions League records did the same. They raised the bar for future players, showing that nothing is out of reach. These achievements became legends, stories that kids would tell on playgrounds, dreaming of one day breaking those records themselves. It's like when someone sets a high score on your favorite arcade game, inspiring you to keep trying until you beat it.

But let's not forget the hard work behind these records. Neither Messi nor Ronaldo just woke up one day and decided to be great. They trained like there was no tomorrow. Imagine waking up before the sun, lacing up your boots, and hitting the field when everyone else is still asleep. That's what it took. They put in hours of practice, refining their skills and pushing their limits. Messi's training involved enhancing his agility and perfecting his dribbling. Ronaldo focused on building his strength and speed, turning himself into a powerhouse on the field. They were committed to being the best versions of themselves every season, never settling for anything less.

Messi's 91 goals in 2012 weren't just about quantity. Each goal was a masterpiece, a testament to his skill and vision. He wasn't just scoring; he was creating art on the field. Every trick, every dribble, every shot was perfectly executed. Ronaldo's consistency in the Champions League was similar. He scored in 11 consecutive games, making it look effortless. His precision and timing were impeccable, leaving defenders in his wake. These moments weren't just about breaking records. They were about showing the world what hard work and dedication could achieve.

Visualize Your Own Goal-Scoring Record

Close your eyes and imagine yourself scoring a goal in your next game. Feel the excitement as the ball hits the net. Now, think about what you need to do to make that dream a reality. Practice your dribbling, work on your shooting, and never give up. Remember, every great player started with a dream, just like you.

Messi and Ronaldo's achievements remind us all that the sky's the limit. Their records aren't just trophies in a cabinet; they're proof that with determination and passion, anything is possible. So, lace up your boots and hit the field. Who knows? Maybe you'll be the next record-breaker in soccer history.

Iconic Matches: Moments of Glory

Picture this: the stadium lights are blinding, the air is buzzing, and the stands are packed with fans who feel like they could explode with excitement. This is El Clásico, the legendary clash between Barcelona and Real Madrid. For Messi, these matches are more than just games. They're like epic battles where he can show off his skills. One unforgettable moment was in 2007, when Messi scored a hat-trick against Real Madrid. It was a day when he seemed unstoppable. With each goal, he weaved through defenders like they were standing still, leaving everyone in awe. It wasn't just about the goals; it was the way he made it look so effortless, like he was playing a casual game in his backyard. That match wasn't just another win for Barcelona. It was Messi's announcement to the world that he was no ordinary player. He was a magician with the ball, ready to take on any challenge.

Now, let's switch to Ronaldo. Imagine him in a Champions League match against Juventus, where he pulled off one of the most jaw-dropping goals of his career. It was an overhead kick that defied gravity. The ball soared into the net, leaving the goalkeeper and fans speechless. Ronaldo's athleticism and precision were on full display. It wasn't just a goal; it was a statement. A moment like this doesn't just happen. It takes years of practice and a whole lot of guts to try something so daring on such a big stage. That goal didn't just win the match; it made headlines across the globe, reminding everyone why Ronaldo was considered one of the best.

These matches did more than just fill highlight reels. They elevated Messi and Ronaldo to global superstar status. After Messi's hat-trick, he became the player everyone wanted to watch. He wasn't just a part of soccer; he was redefining it. His performances in El Clásico weren't just victories for Barcelona. They were victories for soccer fans who cherished the beauty of the game. Ronaldo's overhead kick had a similar impact. It became a viral sensation, shared and replayed by fans everywhere. His ability to shine on such a grand stage influenced both club and international success. It wasn't just about winning trophies; it was about inspiring millions of fans and young players around the world.

But let's not forget the emotions that these matches stirred. The thrill of last-minute goals, the tension in the air, and the eruption of cheers when the ball hits the net. These moments are why fans love the game. They are the heart-stopping instances that make soccer more than just a sport. And then there's the sportsmanship and camaraderie on display. After a hard-fought match, seeing players exchange jerseys and respect is a reminder that, beneath the fierce competition, there's a mutual admiration. It's about more than just winning; it's about celebrating the spirit of the game.

These iconic matches have left a lasting impression on everyone who witnessed them. They aren't just memories; they're legends that will be told and retold for years to come. Messi and Ronaldo have turned countless games into unforgettable experiences. Each match a new chapter in their already illustrious careers. These moments of glory are what make them legends. Each goal, each game, a testament to their skill and passion for soccer. And as long as there are soccer fields and fans, their stories will continue to inspire the next generation.

Awards and Honors: Recognizing Excellence

Imagine standing on a stage, lights shining, cameras flashing, and your name being called as the winner of the most prestigious award in soccer. That's what Lionel Messi and Cristiano Ronaldo have experienced multiple times. One of the highest honors in soccer is the Ballon d'Or. It's like the Oscars for soccer players. Each year, the world waits to see who will take home the golden ball. Messi has won this award a record eight times. Ronaldo isn't far behind with five wins. These aren't just shiny trophies. They're symbols of being recognized as the best in the world by peers, coaches, and journalists who vote for the winner. It's a big deal. It's like being voted as the class president, but on a global scale.

Winning the Ballon d'Or and the FIFA World Player of the Year awards isn't just about having a great season. It's about consistently being at the top of your game. The criteria for these awards involve more than just scoring goals. Players need to show skill, sportsmanship, and influence on the field. It's about how they impact the game and inspire others. The voting process involves people who really know soccer. Coaches, captains, and journalists from around the world cast their votes. This means winning these awards is like getting a high-five from the whole soccer community. They recognize and celebrate the talent and hard work that Messi and Ronaldo bring to the field.

These awards have left a lasting mark on their legacies. Every time Messi or Ronaldo wins, it cements their status as legends. It's like adding another star to their already glittering careers. Consistency is key here. They haven't just won these awards once. They've been recognized over many seasons. This shows that they aren't just one-hit wonders. They're in it for the long haul. Their influence on the game is undeniable. Every time they step onto the field, they bring something special. It's like watching a superhero in action, making impossible things look easy. Their awards are not just personal victories. They're wins for fans, teammates, and the sport itself.

Let's take a moment to talk about their award ceremonies. Picture Messi, standing there, holding the golden ball. When he speaks, he doesn't boast. Instead, he thanks his teammates, coaches, and family. His speeches are full of humility. He knows he couldn't have done it alone. It's like when you win a team relay race and thank everyone who helped you train. Ronaldo's acceptance speeches have their own flair. He often talks about his journey, the sacrifices, and the hard work. He thanks his teammates for their support. He also gives a nod to the fans who cheer him on. It's an acknowledgment that soccer is a team sport, even if the award is individual. Both players make it clear that these moments are shared with everyone who helped them along the way.

These ceremonies aren't just about the awards. They're celebrations of their careers, filled with emotion and gratitude. Messi and Ronaldo remind us that while individual accolades are amazing, it's the support and teamwork that truly matter. The awards are a testament to their greatness, but also to their humility and appreciation for those around them. They show that even at the top, staying grounded and thankful is important.

The stories from these award nights are like tales of triumph. They echo the values of dedication, teamwork, and humility. Whether it's Messi's quiet gratitude or Ronaldo's passionate thanks, their words resonate with fans and players alike. These moments inspire the next generation to dream big, work hard, and always be thankful for the support they receive. They show that even when you reach the pinnacle, you should never forget where you came from and who helped you along the way.

Legacy on the Pitch: Building a Dynasty

When you think about soccer, it's hard not to think about Messi and Ronaldo. Their influence is like a ripple in a pond, spreading far and wide. At their clubs, Messi and Ronaldo did more than just play—they transformed the entire atmosphere. Barcelona, under Messi's dazzling skills, became a powerhouse. The kind of team that struck fear into the hearts of their opponents. It wasn't just about winning games; it was about how they won them. The style, the flair, the grace—Messi turned Barcelona into a team that others wanted to be like. His presence on the field made every match an event. It wasn't just about the goals, but the artistry in how they played.

On the other hand, Ronaldo's time at Real Madrid brought a new era of dominance. It was during his reign that Real Madrid became synonymous with Champions League success. Winning after winning, they became a force no one could ignore. Ronaldo's leadership and drive pushed the team to new heights. His ability to deliver in big moments made Real Madrid a team that was hard to beat. They weren't just a club with a rich history; they were writing new chapters that will be remembered forever. Ronaldo's time there wasn't just about trophies. It was about setting a new standard of excellence.

Their playing styles have left a mark on future generations. Messi, with his incredible dribbling and playmaking skills, has become the gold standard for aspiring midfielders and forwards. Watching him glide past defenders is like watching a magician perform tricks. Young players everywhere try to mimic his moves. They practice tirelessly, hoping to one day have that same touch, that same vision. Messi's style teaches them that soccer isn't just about scoring; it's about creating, about making the impossible look easy.

Ronaldo, on the other hand, is the epitome of physicality and versatility. His strength, speed, and ability to adapt to different roles make him a role model for many. Young athletes look at Ronaldo and see what hard work and dedication can achieve. His workouts and regimen are stuff of legend, inspiring countless youngsters to hit the gym and push their limits. Ronaldo shows them that soccer is as much about physical preparation as it is about skill. He proves that you can be both powerful and technical, a lethal combination on the field.

These legends didn't just dominate games; they led their teams to collective glory. During Messi's era, Barcelona's dominance was clear. They won numerous titles, each one adding to their legacy. The team, guided by Messi's genius, became a model of success. For Ronaldo, his contributions to Real Madrid's Champions League dynasty were immense. They lifted the trophy several times, each victory sweeter than the last. Ronaldo's influence lifted the team, pushing them to achieve great things together. Their success wasn't just individual; it was a shared triumph with teammates.

Beyond the pitch, Messi and Ronaldo have shaped soccer culture and inspired countless young athletes. Their dedication and sportsmanship set examples that resonate worldwide. Kids look up to them, not just for their skills, but for their attitudes. They teach that hard work, humility, and respect are key ingredients to success. Messi and Ronaldo became symbols of what it means to be a true athlete. They inspired young players to dream big, to work hard, and to play fair. Their influence is felt in every corner of the soccer world, from small-town pitches to grand stadiums.

As we wrap up, think about the lasting legacy Messi and Ronaldo leave on soccer. Their impact goes beyond goals and trophies. They changed how the world sees the game, inspiring the next wave of players to reach for the stars. Their stories remind us that greatness isn't just about what you achieve, but how you inspire others along the way.

Chapter 5:

Beyond the Field

Have you ever thought about how soccer is more than just a game? Well, imagine being so good at soccer that you help it become popular around the world. That's exactly what Messi and Ronaldo have done. They aren't just amazing players; they're global ambassadors for soccer. Their influence goes beyond the field. They've played a huge part in spreading the love for soccer to places where it wasn't as popular before. It's like they have a magic soccer wand that makes everyone want to kick a ball around. They've helped the sport grow in new and exciting ways.

Messi and Ronaldo have taken part in international promotional tours. These tours are like world tours for soccer stars, where they visit different countries to promote the sport. Imagine getting to see them play live or even meet them in person. That would be a dream come true for many fans. These tours are a big deal. They help bring attention to soccer in countries where it might not be as popular. They show people how exciting and fun soccer can be. It's like inviting everyone to a giant soccer party, with Messi and Ronaldo as the guests of honor.

They've also been involved in global soccer initiatives. These are projects aimed at making soccer more accessible to everyone. They work with organizations that are dedicated to growing the sport worldwide. This means visiting countries with emerging soccer scenes and helping to boost the sport's popularity. Imagine living in a place where soccer isn't a big deal, and then suddenly, Messi or Ronaldo show up. That would get everyone talking and excited about soccer. They partner with global soccer organizations to make sure the sport reaches every corner of the world. It's like planting soccer seeds in every country and watching them grow into beautiful fields of dreams.

Messi and Ronaldo have also elevated soccer's profile through media appearances and endorsements. They've collaborated with major sports brands, creating lines of gear that fans everywhere can wear. It's like having a piece of their magic with you every time you play. They've even appeared in soccer-themed films and documentaries, sharing their stories and inspiring fans all over. These appearances help people see soccer in a whole new way. It's not just a game; it's a lifestyle. Their involvement in these projects shows how much they love the sport and want to share it with the world.

Their social media accounts are a big part of their global influence. They have millions of followers who hang on to their every post. They use these platforms to engage with fans and create a global soccer community. Imagine getting a like or comment from Messi or Ronaldo on your post. That would be amazing, right? They use social media to advocate for diversity and inclusion in soccer. They want everyone to feel welcome in the sport, no matter where they come from or who they are. They use their platforms to spread positive messages and encourage everyone to play and enjoy soccer.

By being global ambassadors, Messi and Ronaldo have helped soccer become a beloved sport worldwide. They've shown that soccer is more than just a game. It's a way to bring people together, to inspire, and to make a difference. They've used their fame and influence to spread the joy of soccer to every corner of the earth. Their efforts have made soccer a global phenomenon, and they'll continue to inspire future generations to take up the sport and chase their dreams.

Activity: Create Your Own Soccer Promotion Plan

Imagine you're a soccer ambassador like Messi or Ronaldo. How would you promote soccer in your community? Write down three ideas to get more people interested in soccer. Maybe it's organizing a community game, hosting a soccer skills workshop, or starting a local soccer club. Share your ideas with friends and see how you can make them happen. Remember, you have the power to spread the love for soccer, just like Messi and Ronaldo.

5.2 Charitable Endeavors: Giving Back to the Community

Have you ever thought about the power of a helping hand? Messi and Ronaldo certainly have. They don't just play soccer; they make a real difference in the world. Let's start with Messi. He has his own foundation called the Leo Messi Foundation. This isn't just a name. It's a beacon of hope for many children around the world. The foundation focuses on providing health and education to children who need it most. Imagine being a kid who needs medical help but can't afford it. That's where Messi steps in. His foundation helps fund hospitals and clinics, giving kids a chance to get better and grow up strong. It's like he's scoring a goal for every child he helps.

Ronaldo, on the other hand, has a heart as big as his talent. He's known for his efforts in global disaster relief. When disaster strikes, Ronaldo is there to help. He donated a huge sum to help with relief efforts after the earthquake in Nepal. It's like he's saying, "I've got your back," to those in need. His donations provide emergency supplies, medical care, and help rebuild communities. It's more than just money. It's a lifeline for people who have lost everything. He shows that you don't have to be a superhero to save the day. Sometimes, all it takes is a generous spirit and a willingness to help.

Their charitable work is felt both locally and internationally. They've helped build sports facilities in underprivileged areas. These aren't just places to play. They're places where dreams are born. Imagine a kid kicking a ball for the first time on a shiny new field. That's what Messi and Ronaldo have given to so many communities. They also support educational and healthcare initiatives. They believe that every child deserves a shot at a good life, whether it's through learning or staying healthy. Their work has changed lives, turning what seemed impossible into possible. They give hope to those who need it most, lighting up the world one act of kindness at a time.

Messi has teamed up with UNICEF to help kids around the world. Through this partnership, he supports education and protection for children in need. It's like he's building a safety net for them, making sure they have the tools to succeed. Ronaldo's generosity extends to children's hospitals, where he's made significant donations. His contributions help provide care and support to sick kids. Imagine being a child in a hospital and knowing Ronaldo is helping you get better. That's the kind of impact he makes. It's not just about money. It's about showing care and compassion.

So what drives these soccer legends to give back? Personal experiences play a big part. Messi knows what it's like to face challenges. He had a medical condition as a kid and needed treatments to grow. His own struggles inspire him to help others. He wants to make sure no child is left behind. Ronaldo, too, has a story. He grew up in a humble home and knows the value of a helping hand. His background fuels his desire to give back. He remembers what it's like to need support and wants to be that support for others.

Their acts of kindness aren't just headlines. They're real stories with real people behind them. Imagine a young girl who gets the medicine she needs because of Messi's foundation. Picture a family who can rebuild their home after a disaster thanks to Ronaldo's help. These stories are countless and speak volumes about their character. They show that even the biggest stars have the biggest hearts. Their generosity isn't just about giving money. It's about giving hope, love, and a chance for a better tomorrow. They remind us all that no matter how big or small we are, we can all make a difference.

5.3 Role Models for a Generation

Imagine being so good at something that millions of kids around the world look up to you. That's what it's like for Messi and Ronaldo. They're not just superstars on the soccer field; they're role models in life. It's not just about how many goals they score or how many awards they win. It's about how they carry themselves every day. These two legends teach us values like humility and perseverance. They show us that even if you're the best, there's no need to brag or boast. Messi often lets his game do the talking. He doesn't need to shout about his achievements. His quiet confidence speaks volumes. And Ronaldo, with his intense dedication, reminds us that hard work always pays off. These guys keep pushing themselves to be better, even when they've already reached the top.

Through their actions and words, Messi and Ronaldo teach young fans important lessons. They show us the value of hard work and dedication. When you see Ronaldo training long after everyone else has left the field, you understand what it takes to stay at the top. And Messi, with his endless hours on the training ground, proves that practice is key. They also advocate for fair play and sportsmanship. They're always the first to shake hands with their opponents, win or lose. They remind us that respect and kindness are as important as skill and talent. It's not just about winning. It's about playing the game the right way.

Their influence on aspiring athletes and fans is massive. Across the globe, youth soccer programs draw inspiration from their careers. Coaches use videos of Messi and Ronaldo to teach skills and tactics. They become the examples young players strive to follow. You might hear a coach say, "Try dribbling like Messi" or "Aim for goals like Ronaldo." These legends have set a standard for what it means to be a great player and a great person. Young athletes watch and learn, hoping to one day have the same impact. Testimonials from kids who look up to them show how deeply they've touched lives. It's not uncommon to hear a young player say, "I want to be like Messi" or "Ronaldo is my hero."

Handling public scrutiny is another area where they shine. In the spotlight, every move is watched and every mistake magnified. But Messi and Ronaldo show us how to handle criticism with grace. When the media questions Messi's performance, he doesn't lash out. Instead, he focuses on improving, letting his play do the talking. Ronaldo faces his critics head-on, using their words as fuel to drive him forward. They set positive examples in overcoming challenges. When they stumble, they get back up, dust themselves off, and keep going. They teach us that resilience is key and that setbacks are just part of the game.

Their lives off the field are just as inspiring. They balance fame with family, showing that you can be a global icon and still stay grounded. Messi's love for his family is evident in everything he does. He often talks about how important his loved ones are to him. Ronaldo, too, is a family man. He shares moments with his kids and shows that family comes first. This commitment to personal and professional excellence is what makes them true role models. They remind us that no matter how big your dreams are, staying true to yourself and your values is what really matters.

5.4 Shaping Soccer Culture Worldwide

Have you ever noticed how Messi and Ronaldo don't just play soccer? They've become symbols of the sport itself, influencing how people see soccer all over the world. These two are like the north star for fans and players alike. Their impact goes beyond just winning games or scoring goals. They've helped make soccer a global phenomenon, reaching places where it wasn't as popular before. Imagine a country where soccer was once just a pastime, suddenly buzzing with excitement every time these legends step onto the field. They've turned casual onlookers into die-hard fans, all wanting to be a part of the magic.

It's not just their skills on the field that have made waves. Off the field, they've influenced soccer fashion and lifestyle trends, too. Ever spot a cool pair of soccer shoes or a stylish jersey? Chances are, Messi or Ronaldo had something to do with it. They've partnered with brands to create gear that fans can wear, making everyone feel like they're part of the game. Their styles set the bar high, not just for looks but for performance, too. It's like they've made soccer a part of everyday life, not just something you watch on TV.

When it comes to evolving playing styles, Messi and Ronaldo are in a league of their own. Messi's dribbling is like poetry in motion. He weaves through defenders as if they're not even there. Watching him play, you might think he's inventing new moves on the spot. Then there's Ronaldo, who combines power and precision in ways that seem almost superhuman. His ability to score from impossible angles has inspired coaches to rethink strategies and training methods. They don't just stick to the old ways. They innovate and adapt, showing that soccer is an ever-evolving game, and there's always room for new ideas.

Their influence extends to social and cultural discussions. They've used their platforms to speak up for social change, showing that soccer can be a powerful tool for good. Whether it's standing against discrimination or advocating for equality, they're not afraid to use their voices. They remind us that soccer isn't just about what's on the field. It's about the values it promotes and the community it builds. Their involvement in these conversations underscores the role of soccer in cultural identity. It's a sport that belongs to everyone, and they've shown that it can be a force for unity and positive change.

Now, let's talk about the next generation. Messi and Ronaldo have inspired countless young players to pick up a soccer ball and dream big. They host youth soccer camps and workshops, where kids learn not just skills but the spirit of the game. Imagine being a young athlete, kicking a ball around at a camp hosted by one of your heroes. It's a chance to learn from the best and see up close what dedication looks like. These camps are more than just training sessions. They're experiences that shape future stars, teaching them the importance of teamwork, resilience, and passion.

Their stories serve as powerful motivation for young athletes everywhere. Kids hear about Messi's humble beginnings in Rosario or Ronaldo's relentless drive in Madeira and think, "If they can do it, so can I." These tales of perseverance and success light a fire in the hearts of aspiring players, encouraging them to chase their dreams no matter the odds. It's not just about becoming the next Messi or Ronaldo, though. It's about finding your unique path and putting in the effort to make your dreams a reality. Their legacies remind us all that with grit and determination, anything is possible.

Messi and Ronaldo's influence is like a ripple effect, spreading across continents and cultures, leaving a lasting impact wherever they go. Their contributions to the sport have transcended the field, shaping how soccer is played, watched, and loved worldwide. They've shown us that soccer is more than just a game. It's a way of life that connects people, inspires change, and builds a community. As we look to the future, their legacy will continue to inspire new generations, proving that the beautiful game truly has the power to change the world.

Chapter 6:

The Personal Side of Greatness

Ever thought about what it would be like to be famous? Now imagine being famous across the entire planet. Sounds cool, right? But here's the catch—being famous isn't just about signing autographs and smiling for the cameras. It's a whole different game, especially when you're someone like Lionel Messi or Cristiano Ronaldo. These soccer legends don't just deal with defenders on the pitch; they also face the spotlight 24/7. Fame can be like a double-edged sword. On one hand, it brings amazing opportunities and recognition. On the other hand, it makes keeping a private life a real challenge.

For Messi and Ronaldo, privacy is as rare as a unicorn. The media and paparazzi follow them everywhere, snapping photos and asking questions at all hours. It's like living in a fishbowl, with the world peering in. Imagine going out for ice cream and finding a dozen cameras pointed at you. Not exactly a peaceful day out, right? This constant attention makes it tough to keep family life private. Both Messi and Ronaldo have to work hard to shield their loved ones from the public eye. They want their families to have normal lives, away from the chaos that fame can bring. And that's no easy task.

To manage this, they have some clever strategies up their sleeves. Messi and Ronaldo make sure to schedule family vacations and retreats. These trips are a chance to escape the spotlight and just be themselves. Imagine hanging out on a beach with your family, building sandcastles and playing soccer without a single camera in sight. It's a chance to recharge and connect with the people who matter most. They also set boundaries between their public and private lives. It's like drawing a line in the sand, making sure that when they're with family, they're fully present. This helps them focus on what really counts, even when the world is watching.

Family support is like the secret sauce that keeps them going. Messi and Ronaldo both lean on their families for emotional support. Whether it's a hug from their kids after a tough match or words of encouragement from their spouses, these moments remind them of where they came from. It keeps them grounded and motivated. Their families also play a big role in their personal and professional decisions. Imagine having a team of people who always have your back, cheering you on no matter what. That's what family is all about, and it's a big part of why Messi and Ronaldo can handle the pressures of fame.

Messi and Ronaldo also use their platforms to share family values with their fans. They often post on social media, showcasing sweet family moments. These posts are like little windows into their world, showing the love and laughter that make life special. It's a reminder that behind the fame, they're just like anyone else. They also make public appearances with their families, showing that family comes first. Whether it's attending a charity event or cheering from the sidelines, these moments highlight the importance of having loved ones by their side.

Reflection Section: Your Own Family Time

Think about your own family and how you spend time together. What activities bring you closer? Write down three fun things you can do as a family this week. It could be playing a game, going for a walk, or having a movie night. Remember, it's not about what you do, but the time you spend together that counts.

Messi and Ronaldo's stories remind us that even in the whirlwind of fame, family is the anchor that keeps us steady. Their efforts to protect and prioritize their families show that true greatness isn't just about winning on the field—it's about cherishing the people who make life meaningful.

Personal Sacrifices: What It Takes to Be the Best

Imagine being invited to the biggest birthday party of the year, but you have to skip it because you need to train. That's the kind of sacrifice Lionel Messi and Cristiano Ronaldo have made for as long as they can remember. Their lives are like a never-ending soccer match, where every decision could make or break their careers. Missing family events, birthdays, and even holidays is part of their routine. Imagine saying goodbye to your family on Christmas Eve to catch a flight for a match. It's all because they have a commitment to their sport that goes beyond personal desires. They know that being the best means making tough choices, even if it means missing out on special moments with loved ones.

Both Messi and Ronaldo stick to strict diets and fitness routines. Think about all the times you've reached for a cookie or a slice of pizza. For these guys, it's different. They follow meal plans that are as precise as a math formula. Every calorie is counted, every meal planned. They can't just eat whatever is in the fridge. It's all about staying in peak physical condition. They train harder than anyone else, often working out when everyone else is asleep. They lift weights, run miles, and practice for hours. It's a level of dedication that most people can't even imagine. It's like they're on a mission, and nothing—no matter how tempting—can get in their way.

But let's not forget the emotional and psychological toll these sacrifices take. Being away from family and friends can be lonely. Picture yourself in a hotel room, thousands of miles from home, while everyone you care about is together. That's a reality Messi and Ronaldo face constantly. They miss out on creating memories with their families, and it can get pretty lonely. There's also the pressure to live up to their own expectations. With every goal they score, the bar gets set higher. It's like having a shadow that never leaves, always reminding them they can't afford to fail. This pressure can be overwhelming. Some days, it must feel like the weight of the world is resting on their shoulders.

There are times when personal desires must take a backseat to professional obligations. Imagine being invited to your best friend's wedding, but knowing you have to skip it because of an important match. Both Messi and Ronaldo have faced moments like these. They have had to turn down invites to milestone celebrations because their careers demanded it. It's not easy, but they understand that sacrifices are necessary to reach the top. They know that in order to achieve their dreams, they have to make choices that others might not understand. They've learned to prioritize their careers, even when their hearts might want something different.

Despite the sacrifices, the rewards are enormous. Achieving career goals and breaking records is a feeling like no other. When Messi holds up a trophy or Ronaldo scores a record-breaking goal, the sacrifices seem worth it. They inspire millions around the world through their dedication and commitment. Young athletes look up to them, dreaming of following in their footsteps. It's a reminder that hard work pays off. They show that with discipline and perseverance, anything is possible. Their stories are proof that sacrifices can lead to incredible rewards.

The fulfillment they get from their careers goes beyond personal achievements. They have become symbols of hope and inspiration. Their stories of sacrifice and success tell us that it's not just about talent. It's about the hours spent practicing, the meals skipped, and the parties missed. It's about doing what it takes to be the best. For Messi and Ronaldo, it's not just about soccer. It's about leaving a legacy that will inspire generations to come.

Handling Criticism: Staying Grounded

Imagine being Messi or Ronaldo for a moment. You're out there on the field, pouring your heart into every kick, every pass, and every goal. But no matter how well you play, there are always critics. The media loves to pick apart their performances, analyzing every little mistake. It's like having a giant magnifying glass hovering over them, ready to catch any slip-up. One missed goal or a less-than-perfect game, and it's all over the headlines. Reporters and commentators debate their form, questioning if they've lost their spark. It's a lot of pressure, knowing that any game could spark a media frenzy. Off the field, they face scrutiny for their personal choices too. Whether it's a new endorsement or a change in their personal lives, people always have opinions. They can't even wear a new outfit without someone commenting on it. For Messi and Ronaldo, handling this constant criticism is just part of the job.

But how do they manage to keep their heads up amid all this noise? Well, they have their ways. They focus on the constructive feedback that can actually help them improve. Think of it like when a coach gives you tips after a game. You listen, you learn, and you get better. Messi and Ronaldo do the same. They sift through the noise to find the valuable nuggets of advice. They also develop a thick skin against the negative comments. It's like putting on armor that shields them from the hurtful words. They know that not every opinion matters. They focus on what truly counts: their own goals and the support of those who believe in them. Over time, they've learned to separate the helpful criticism from the useless chatter.

Criticism has actually fueled their growth. It's like adding fuel to a fire. For Ronaldo, early career doubts were a big challenge. Some people thought he was too flashy, all show and no substance. But instead of letting it bring him down, he used it as motivation. He trained harder, determined to prove everyone wrong. His response was simple: let his game do the talking. He turned doubts into victories, showing the world that he was more than just hype. Messi faced criticism about his leadership skills. Some said he wasn't vocal enough on the field. Instead of ignoring it, Messi used this feedback to evolve. He worked on his communication and presence, becoming a leader in his own quiet way. These challenges pushed them to grow and improve, turning criticism into a catalyst for success.

Mentors and confidantes play a big role in helping Messi and Ronaldo navigate criticism. They have trusted figures who offer advice and guidance. It's like having a wise coach who knows just what to say when you're feeling down. These mentors remind them of their strengths and keep them grounded. They help them see the big picture, putting things into perspective. A strong support network, like a circle of friends and family, also helps. These are the people who believe in them unconditionally, who remind them of their worth when doubts creep in. They provide a safe space to vent, laugh, and recharge. With their help, Messi and Ronaldo can face criticism with confidence and keep moving forward.

The ability to handle criticism is one of the many things that set Messi and Ronaldo apart. It's not just about brushing off the negativity. It's about knowing when to listen, when to ignore, and when to use it as fuel to get better. They stay focused on what truly matters: their passion for the game, their personal goals, and the people who support them. They teach us all that while criticism is unavoidable, it doesn't define who we are. It's just noise. What truly defines us are our actions, our determination, and our ability to rise above.

The Importance of Humility in Success

Humility might seem like a rare trait for superstars, but for Messi and Ronaldo, it's key. These two aren't just admired for their skills on the pitch. They're also respected for how they carry themselves. Imagine winning award after award and still giving credit to your teammates. That's how Messi and Ronaldo roll. They know soccer isn't a one-man show. Each time they stand on that podium, they make sure to thank those who helped them get there. It's like saying, "Hey, I couldn't have done this without you!" This kind of recognition shows that they value every goal, every assist, every bit of hard work put in by their teammates. It's not just about them; it's about the whole team. Their modest behavior during award ceremonies is a testament to their humility. They don't make it all about themselves. Instead, they share the spotlight with others. It's a powerful reminder that even the greatest players know they didn't get there alone.

This down-to-earth attitude has won them fans worldwide. People love them not just for their talent but for their genuine interactions. Messi and Ronaldo take time to engage with fans and communities. Whether it's signing autographs or visiting schools, they make others feel valued. You can see it in their eyes when they meet a young fan. They listen, they laugh, and they share a moment that feels real. These interactions show that they're not just icons; they're people who care. Their respect extends to opponents and colleagues too. They play hard but fair. They shake hands after a match, win or lose, showing that respect and sportsmanship matter.

There are plenty of examples where their humility shines through. Messi, for instance, never hypes up his personal achievements. Even after scoring a hat-trick, he remains humble. He focuses on what the team accomplished rather than his own stats. It's like he's saying, "This isn't just my win; it's ours." Ronaldo is similar.

He often praises other players' successes. He doesn't shy away from acknowledging the talents of others. By doing so, he shows that even the best can appreciate greatness in others. They teach us that humility isn't about downplaying your success. It's about recognizing the efforts of others and staying grounded no matter how high you climb.

These humble gestures teach valuable lessons. They encourage teamwork and collaboration. They show that working together is what makes a team strong. Messi and Ronaldo inspire young athletes to lift each other up. They emphasize that success is sweeter when it's shared. They also highlight the importance of staying grounded despite success. No matter how many goals they score, they never forget where they came from. They remind us that true greatness isn't just about what you achieve. It's about how you treat others and the legacy you leave behind. Their humility sets a standard for aspiring players everywhere.

As we wrap up this chapter, it's clear that humility is more than just a trait for Messi and Ronaldo. It's a way of life. Their actions on and off the field show that being humble doesn't make you weak. It makes you strong. It earns you respect and admiration from fans, peers, and even rivals. Humility helps them connect with people from all walks of life. It makes them relatable, reminding us that they are human too. As we look to the next chapter, let's keep in mind that success isn't just about reaching the top. It's about lifting others up with you and staying true to yourself.

Chapter 7:

The Art of Mastery

Imagine you're playing soccer with your friends, and suddenly, you have the ball. Everyone's eyes are on you. The defenders close in, and for a split second, you feel like you're in a video game. Your heart races. You want to do something incredible, something they'll talk about all week. That's the magic of dribbling, and nobody does it better than Lionel Messi. When we talk about Messi's dribbling, it's like discussing how a magician pulls off his best tricks. It's not just about skill; it's about creating moments that leave everyone speechless.

Messi's dribbling is a masterpiece of control and precision. His secret? A low center of gravity. At 5'7", Messi is like a sports car on a winding road. He can change directions faster than you can say "goal." This low center lets him zip past defenders with ease. He doesn't just run past them; he dances. His feet move in a blur, each touch of the ball perfectly timed. You might think he's going right, and then—boom—he's gone left. It's like watching a cat toy with a ball of yarn, never losing control, always one step ahead.

What makes Messi truly special is his ability to use short, rapid touches. Imagine tapping a balloon, just enough to keep it from hitting the ground. That's how Messi handles the ball. Each touch is light and deliberate, almost like he's playing a gentle game of keep-away. This technique lets him navigate through defenders like they're cones on a practice field. With short touches, he keeps the ball close, making it nearly impossible for opponents to snatch it away. His feet are always busy, shifting and adjusting, making defenders dizzy as they try to keep up. The ball seems glued to his feet, and he controls it with the finesse of a master craftsman.

But it's not just about fancy footwork. Messi uses his whole body to outmaneuver opponents. He's a master of feints and body swerves. Picture this: he glances one way, makes a quick shift with his hips, and suddenly he's in the clear. It's like watching a magician misdirect the audience. One moment you're sure he's going to pass, and the next, he's slipped through a tiny gap. These moves leave defenders chasing shadows. His feints are subtle, yet devastatingly effective, causing even the best defenders to stumble. It's all about misdirection, making them think they know his next move, when really, they have no clue.

Messi's dribbling also relies on exceptional peripheral vision. It's like he has eyes on the back of his head. He sees the whole field without losing focus on the ball. This vision allows him to anticipate defenders' movements, finding gaps before they even materialize. It's like playing chess three steps ahead. When you watch him play, you see how he reads the game, making split-second decisions that change everything. He can spot a defender's weight shift and use it to his advantage, slipping past them with ease. It's a skill that lets him exploit the tiniest of openings, turning potential dead ends into opportunities.

Some of Messi's most iconic moments come from his dribbling genius. Remember that solo goal against Getafe? He picked up the ball in his own half, took on half the opposing team, and scored a goal that left everyone in awe. Or the time against Real Madrid when he danced through the defense, leaving world-class players in his wake. These moments aren't just highlights; they're history. His dribbling has led to countless game-winning assists and goals that have become legendary. Watching him dribble is like watching an artist at work, each movement a brushstroke on the canvas of the game.

So, you might be wondering, how can you dribble like Messi? Well, it starts with practicing close ball control. Set up some cones and practice weaving in and out, using both feet. Focus on keeping the ball close, just like Messi does. Try the three-cone tight space dribbling drill. Set up three cones in a triangle and practice weaving through them. Use different parts of your foot and keep your head up. This drill will help you develop better control and confidence with the ball.

Agility training is also key. Work on quick direction changes and balance. Set up an obstacle course and practice moving through it as quickly as possible. The more you train, the more comfortable you'll become with the ball at your feet. And remember, it's not about being perfect. It's about improving a little bit every day. So, lace up those boots, hit the field, and start practicing. Who knows? Maybe one day, you'll be mesmerizing defenders with your own dribbling magic.

Ronaldo's Power and Precision

Imagine you're watching a storm and suddenly, lightning strikes. That's what it's like when Cristiano Ronaldo charges down the field. His style isn't just about power; it's also about precision. Ronaldo combines these elements in a way that leaves defenders confused and goalkeepers guessing. His explosive pace is one of his most feared weapons. The moment he gets the ball, he accelerates like a rocket. Defenders often see him as a blur, unable to keep up. This speed gives him an edge, allowing him to find spaces that others can't even see. It's not just about running fast; it's about knowing when to burst into action, catching everyone off guard. His pace is matched by his precision. Whether he's shooting or passing, Ronaldo has a knack for making the ball go exactly where he wants. His shots are laser-focused, hitting targets with the accuracy of a master archer. This combination of speed and accuracy makes him a constant threat on the field.

But what makes Ronaldo capable of such feats? It's not just natural talent; it's the result of intense physical training. Ronaldo's commitment to fitness is legendary. He's like a superhero, always working to improve his strength and endurance. He spends countless hours in the gym, building a body that's both powerful and agile. His training focuses on strength conditioning, ensuring every muscle contributes to his performance. Ronaldo's legs are like coiled springs, ready to unleash energy at a moment's notice. His fitness regime is matched by his jump training. Watching Ronaldo leap for a header is like seeing a basketball player go for a slam dunk. He seems to hang in the air, defying gravity, and his aerial ability is second to none. This skill allows him to score crucial headers, often in the most challenging situations. His physical attributes aren't just about looking strong; they're about being strong, and they give him the edge to dominate the field.

Ronaldo's power and precision have changed the course of many matches. Who can forget his long-range strikes that left goalkeepers rooted to the spot? It's like watching a cannonball soar through the air, unstoppable and destined for glory. These goals are more than just points on a scoreboard; they're moments of magic that leave fans in awe. His ability to score from distance keeps defenders on their toes, knowing that any lapse in concentration could lead to a spectacular goal. Then there are his headers in tightly contested matches. It's like watching a chess master make the perfect move, turning the tide in his favor. Ronaldo's timing and positioning are impeccable, allowing him to capitalize on the slightest opening. These moments demonstrate not only his skill but also his ability to rise to the occasion, delivering when it matters most.

So, how can you develop your own power and precision? It starts with strength and conditioning programs. Focus on building your core and leg strength. Exercises like squats and lunges can help you build the power you need. Don't forget agility drills, which can improve your speed and balance. Practice shooting accuracy with different techniques. Use cones to set targets and work on hitting them consistently. Try different types of shots, like volleys and low drives, to see what works best for you. Remember, practice makes perfect. Repetition helps develop muscle memory, allowing your body to perform almost automatically in high-pressure situations. It's not just about kicking the ball hard; it's about knowing where you want it to go and making it happen.

Ronaldo's journey to greatness wasn't an overnight success. It took dedication, hard work, and a commitment to constant improvement. He shows us that with the right mindset and training, you can achieve incredible things. Next time you step onto the field, think about how you can incorporate power and precision into your game. Whether it's a powerful shot or a precise pass, remember that you're capable of greatness. Ronaldo's story is proof that with effort and determination, you can turn your dreams into reality.

Mastering the Free Kick

Picture this: a wall of defenders stands tall, the crowd hushes, and the goalie is on high alert. It's a free kick moment, and everyone knows something magical is about to happen. Messi and Ronaldo have turned these moments into art forms. Each takes a different approach, yet both have perfected the free kick in ways that leave spectators in awe. Messi's technique is all about the curl. When he lines up a free kick, there's a sense of calm. Then, with a graceful strike, the ball bends like a whisper, finding the top corner of the net. It's like he's painting with his foot, each curve a brushstroke. The finesse and accuracy are mind-boggling. It's not just power, but precision. He knows exactly how to make the ball dance in the air, teasing the goalie before nestling into the net. Ronaldo, meanwhile, uses the knuckleball technique. It's unpredictable and thrilling. The ball seems to defy physics, wobbling mid-air like it has a mind of its own. It keeps goalies guessing, shifting direction at the last moment. One second, the ball looks headed straight; the next, it's swerving unexpectedly. This unpredictability gives Ronaldo an edge, making each free kick an adventure.

Practice is the backbone of mastering free kicks. Messi and Ronaldo didn't just wake up with these skills. They spent countless hours perfecting them. They experimented with different angles and distances, like scientists in a lab. You can't just kick the ball and hope for the best. You have to understand how it moves. Try setting up varied practice scenarios. Start close to the goal, then gradually move back. Play around with the placement of the ball. See how it affects the curl or wobble. Try new spins and see what happens. It's like solving a puzzle, where each piece needs to fit just right. Through trial and error, you'll learn what works best for you. It's all about finding your own rhythm and style.

Some free kick goals are unforgettable. Messi's free kick against Liverpool in the Champions League was a masterpiece. The ball soared over the wall, curving perfectly into the top corner. The goalie stretched in vain, helpless against the precision of Messi's strike. It was a goal that left fans speechless, a moment that will live in soccer history. Ronaldo's free kick against Spain in the World Cup was equally iconic. With the game on the line, he stepped up with confidence. The ball flew with power and dipped into the net, leaving everyone in awe. It was a clutch moment, showcasing Ronaldo's ability to deliver when it matters most. These goals weren't just about skill. They were about courage and the willingness to take risks.

If you want to improve your free kick skills, focus on consistency. It's about doing the same thing over and over until it becomes second nature. Repetition is key. Spend time getting to know how your foot strikes the ball. Analyze professional routines for inspiration. Watch videos of Messi and Ronaldo. See how they approach the ball and how their body moves. Notice their foot placement and follow-through. Try to incorporate these techniques into your practice. But remember, it's not about copying them exactly. It's about finding what works for you and making it your own. Everyone's style is unique.

Think of free kick practice like a fun challenge. Set up targets in the goal to aim for. Start with larger targets, then make them smaller as you improve. Challenge yourself to hit specific spots. Track your progress and celebrate small victories. Each time you hit the target, you're one step closer to mastering the free kick. It's about patience and persistence. Don't be discouraged if you don't get it right away. Even the best had to start somewhere. Keep practicing, keep experimenting, and most importantly, keep believing in yourself.

Footwork and Finishing: The Ultimate Skills

When it comes to footwork and finishing, Messi and Ronaldo turn soccer into a kind of art. Each has their own style, but both are masters at making the ball do exactly what they want. Messi's footwork inside the box is like a ballet performance. He uses deft touches that seem almost magical. With the ball at his feet, he can glide through the tightest defenses. It's all about timing and control. He waits for the perfect moment to strike, and when he does, it's like the ball knows exactly where it's supposed to go. His finesse in these moments is unmatched. He doesn't just shoot; he places the ball exactly where he wants it. It's like he's playing chess, always thinking a few moves ahead.

Ronaldo, on the other hand, brings a different kind of magic. His quick pivots and volleys are a sight to behold. Picture this: the ball comes flying through the air, and with one swift movement,

Ronaldo connects perfectly, sending it crashing into the net. His ability to change direction quickly and unleash powerful volleys makes him a constant threat. It's not just brute force; there's a precision to it. His footwork allows him to adjust on the fly, making split-second decisions that often result in spectacular goals. Whether it's a tap-in or a thunderous strike, Ronaldo's finishing is both powerful and precise. His quick thinking in these situations is what sets him apart.

Their finishing skills have made them legends. Messi's composure in one-on-one situations is a thing of beauty. Imagine standing there with only the goalie to beat. The pressure is on, but Messi stays calm. He sizes up the situation, picks his spot, and delivers with pinpoint accuracy. It's like he has ice in his veins. He's not just aiming; he's executing a plan. His placement is so precise that even the best goalies struggle to stop him. Meanwhile, Ronaldo's ability to score from various angles and positions is legendary. He can find the net from almost anywhere. Whether it's a tight angle or a crowded box, he makes it work. His versatility in front of the goal is second to none. He knows exactly how to find that tiny gap and exploit it.

You might wonder how their footwork and finishing can change a game. Well, let's revisit some of their clutch moments. Messi's intricate footwork often leads to goals in the most crowded defenses. It's like watching a magician pull off a trick, and nobody knows how he did it. He weaves through the chaos, finding space where there seems to be none. It's like he's playing with a cheat code, able to unlock defenses at will. These moments turn games on their heads, shifting momentum in his team's favor. Ronaldo's clinical finishes in high-pressure situations are just as impactful. Picture a tense match with everything on the line. Ronaldo steps up and delivers, finding the back of the net when it matters most. His ability to keep cool and execute in these moments defines him. He's like a fearless warrior, always ready to seize the moment and change the course of the game.

To develop your own footwork and finishing, start with drills that focus on quick foot movements. Set up cones and practice moving in and out with speed and precision. This will help you build the agility and control needed for those tight situations. Work on shot placement by aiming for specific targets in the goal. Adjust your position and practice hitting different spots. The more you practice, the more natural it will feel. Try different finishing scenarios to improve adaptability. Simulate game conditions with a friend or coach. Practice shooting from various angles and distances. This will help you become comfortable with different situations. The key is to stay relaxed and focused, just like Messi and Ronaldo do.

Footwork and finishing are the ultimate skills in soccer. They're what turn good players into great ones. With dedication and practice, you can improve and reach new heights. Remember, every great player started where you are now. They worked hard, practiced relentlessly, and never stopped dreaming. So, keep pushing yourself and stay committed. The field is your canvas, and with the right skills, you can create your own masterpiece. The next chapter will explore how teamwork and leadership play a crucial role in soccer success.

Chapter 8:

Teamwork and Leadership

Ever wonder what makes someone a great leader? Is it a loud voice that commands attention, or is it the quiet strength that moves mountains without a sound? In the soccer world, leadership isn't just about wearing the captain's armband. It's about inspiring your team, leading them through the highs and lows, and making everyone believe that anything is possible. Messi and Ronaldo, two of the greatest soccer players, have mastered this art, each in their own unique way. Their leadership styles are as different as night and day, yet both are equally effective. Let's dive into how these legends lead their teams and inspire greatness on and off the field.

8.1 Leading by Example: Captains on and Off the Field

Messi's leadership style is a testament to the power of quiet influence. He doesn't need to shout or make grand gestures to get his point across. Instead, he leads through his actions and his unwavering dedication to the game. Think of him as the silent hero in your favorite movie—the one who always comes through when it matters most. His teammates know they can rely on him to deliver exceptional performances, and this consistency inspires them to push their own limits. Messi sets the bar high, not just with his skills, but with his work ethic. He shows that true leadership isn't about being the loudest in the room, but about being the most committed. His presence alone can rally his team, like when he led Barcelona in a stunning comeback win. His calm confidence under pressure gives his teammates the belief that they can achieve the impossible, even when the odds are stacked against them.

On the flip side, Ronaldo's leadership style is full of energy and enthusiasm. He's the kind of captain who rallies his team with passionate speeches and a never-say-die attitude. Picture a coach who can motivate you to run that extra mile or do one more push-up when you think you can't. That's Ronaldo. His vocal and motivational style lifts the spirits of his teammates, reminding them of their potential. He knows that words have power, and he uses them to fuel his team's drive to succeed. Ronaldo's ability to inspire confidence is evident in moments like the Euro 2016 final, where he motivated Portugal to victory despite being injured. His passion is infectious, and it brings out the best in his team. Ronaldo doesn't just talk the talk; he walks the walk, leading by example with his tireless work ethic and commitment to excellence.

Leading by example has a profound impact on team performance and morale. When you see your captain putting in the hard yards, it makes you want to do the same. It sets a standard that everyone strives to meet, creating a culture of dedication and perseverance. Messi's quiet leadership encourages his teammates to focus on the task at hand and trust in their abilities. His influence fosters a sense of calm and composure, even in the most intense situations. Ronaldo's vocal leadership, on the other hand, creates an atmosphere of confidence and determination. His energy lifts the team's spirits and reminds them that they're capable of achieving greatness.

For young athletes looking to adopt leadership qualities, there's much to learn from these icons. Start by encouraging your teammates through your own actions. Show them what hard work and dedication look like, both during practice and in games. Maintain your composure and focus, even when things don't go your way. Remember, leadership isn't about being perfect; it's about showing resilience and determination. Lead by example, whether it's by staying late to practice or by supporting a teammate who's having a tough day. Your actions will speak volumes, and they'll inspire those around you to do the same.

Reflective Exercise: The Role Model in You

Think of a time when you inspired someone by your actions. It could be as simple as helping a teammate or staying positive during a challenging game. Write down what you did and how it made you feel. Then, set a goal to continue leading by example, just like Messi and Ronaldo. Reflect on how you can inspire others and create a positive impact on your team. Remember, leadership isn't about being in charge. It's about taking care of those in your charge and lifting them up when they need it the most.

8.2 Building Chemistry with Teammates

Have you ever played a game of soccer and just clicked with your teammates? Like, you pass the ball, and it feels like they're reading your mind, knowing exactly where to be. That's what building chemistry with teammates is all about. It's those moments when everything just flows, and you're not just playing a game; you're creating something amazing together. Messi and Ronaldo are masters at this, and it's a huge reason why they've been so successful. They know that soccer isn't a solo act. It's a team effort, and building strong relationships with teammates is key to making that happen.

Messi has this incredible ability to connect with his teammates on the field. It's like he has an invisible string that ties them all together. He knows where his teammates are, even without looking. This connection allows him to make those perfect passes that seem impossible to everyone else. His chemistry with players like Xavi and Iniesta was legendary. They understood each other so well that it was like watching a dance. Every pass, every move was in sync. Messi's play is all about collaboration. He's not just looking to score himself; he's looking to create opportunities for his teammates. His unselfish assists are a testament to that. He knows that when the team succeeds, everyone succeeds. It's a beautiful thing to watch, and it shows how important it is to have that intuitive connection with your teammates.

Ronaldo, on the other hand, has a knack for integrating with new teams and players. He's played in several top leagues, and each time, he's managed to fit right in. This isn't by accident. Ronaldo makes a conscious effort to communicate and coordinate with his teammates. He knows that to be successful, he needs to understand how his teammates play and how he can complement their skills. His partnerships with players like Benzema and Modrić are proof of this. They've created some magical moments on the field, and it all comes down to their ability to work together seamlessly. Ronaldo's communication during plays is key. He's always talking, always directing, always making sure everyone is on the same page. It's this constant communication that builds trust and understanding, laying the groundwork for great teamwork.

Messi and Ronaldo's partnerships with their teammates are the stuff of legend. Messi's synergy with Xavi and Iniesta was something special. It was like they shared one soccer brain. Their quick passes and fluid movements made it nearly impossible for opponents to keep up. They knew each other's strengths and played to them, creating a style of play that was both beautiful and effective. Ronaldo's partnerships with Benzema and Modrić have been just as impactful. They've created some unforgettable moments, combining Ronaldo's flair with Benzema's precision and Modrić's creativity. These partnerships highlight the importance of understanding your teammates and working together to achieve a common goal.

So, how can you build effective team chemistry like Messi and Ronaldo? It starts with communication. Open communication channels are crucial. Talk to your teammates on and off the field. Understand their strengths and weaknesses and find ways to support each other. Don't be afraid to speak up and share your thoughts. Remember, you're all working towards the same goal. Participating in team-building activities can also help. Whether it's a simple game of tag or a group exercise, these activities can strengthen bonds and improve teamwork. They're a fun way to get to know your teammates better and build trust.

Building chemistry with teammates isn't just about winning games. It's about creating a supportive environment where everyone feels valued and included. It's about lifting each other up and working together to achieve greatness. Just like Messi and Ronaldo, you can create something amazing with your teammates by building strong relationships and fostering a sense of unity. So, get out there, communicate, and work together to make magic happen on the field.

8.3 Team Dynamics: The Importance of Unity

Imagine being part of a team where everyone works together like a well-oiled machine. That's the power of unity. When a team is united, it's like having a secret weapon. Everyone knows their role, and they're all working towards the same goal. This collective effort is what makes a team successful. It's not about one player shining bright. It's about everyone playing their part. Think of a soccer match where each player knows exactly where to be and what to do. They pass the ball, cover for each other, and celebrate every goal together. That's unity in action. When a team is united, they can overcome any challenge. They can win against the odds and achieve great things together.

Unity isn't just about playing well. It's about handling conflicts too. Every team faces disagreements. Maybe someone doesn't pass the ball enough, or someone takes too many shots. But a united team knows how to deal with these issues. They talk it out, listen to each other, and find solutions. They don't let small problems become big ones. Instead, they work together to create a positive environment. This makes everyone feel valued and respected. A team that handles conflicts well is a team that's ready for any challenge. They know that differences make them stronger, not weaker. They embrace each other's strengths and support each other's weaknesses. This creates a team that's not just good, but great.

Messi plays a huge role in maintaining harmony within his squad. He's like the glue that holds everyone together. He knows that a happy team is a successful team. So, he makes sure everyone feels included and appreciated. He listens to his teammates and values their opinions. He knows that everyone has something to contribute. This attitude creates a sense of belonging and trust. His calm demeanor helps keep the peace, even in tense situations. When Messi is on the field, his teammates know they can rely on him. His presence reassures them, and his actions inspire them to give their best. This creates a team that's not just united, but unstoppable.

Ronaldo, on the other hand, lifts his teammates through encouragement. He's like a cheerleader on the field, always motivating and uplifting others. He knows that everyone plays better when they feel confident. So, he makes sure everyone knows they're important. He praises their efforts and celebrates their successes. He knows that a pat on the back can go a long way. His positive energy is contagious, and it boosts team morale. Ronaldo's encouragement creates a supportive environment where everyone feels valued. This makes his team more resilient and ready to face any challenge. When Ronaldo is on the field, his teammates feel inspired to push their limits and achieve greatness together.

Team unity has led to some extraordinary achievements. Take Barcelona's triumphs in the Champions League, for example. Their success wasn't just about individual talent. It was about the team working together as one. The players trusted each other and played with a shared purpose. They knew that every pass, every tackle, and every goal was a team effort. This unity made them a force to be reckoned with. The same goes for Portugal's unexpected victory at the European Championship. It was a testament to what a united team can achieve. They faced tough opponents, but their determination and teamwork saw them through. These achievements show that when a team is united, they can achieve the impossible.

For young players looking to enhance unity within their own teams, there are several strategies to consider. Start by emphasizing common goals. Make sure everyone knows what they're working towards. When everyone has the same vision, it's easier to work together. Encourage respect and collaboration among teammates. Show that everyone's contribution matters. Celebrate each other's successes and support each other through challenges. Create opportunities for team bonding. Whether it's a team dinner or a fun activity, these moments can strengthen relationships and build trust. Remember, a united team is a strong team. By working together and supporting each other, you can achieve great things both on and off the field.

8.4 Leadership Styles: Inspiring Others

Have you ever noticed how some leaders make you feel like you can do anything, while others push you to strive for your best? Messi and Ronaldo each have their own unique ways of inspiring those around them. Messi leads with empathy and support. He understands his teammates on a personal level. He knows when they need encouragement and when they need space. His approach is like a gentle breeze, guiding his team without overwhelming them. He listens, he cares, and he uses his understanding to bring out the best in everyone. This empathetic style creates a family-like atmosphere where everyone feels valued and motivated to excel. Messi's leadership is about lifting others up, showing them that their contributions matter. It's a style that resonates with those who value connection and understanding.

Ronaldo, on the other hand, is all about charisma and assertiveness. He's like a spark that ignites the team. His energy is contagious, and he knows how to get everyone fired up. His presence commands attention and respect. Ronaldo's leadership style is bold and direct. He sets high standards and challenges his teammates to meet them. His assertiveness pushes them to go beyond their limits, to reach for greatness. He knows that a little pressure can bring out the best in people. His charismatic nature inspires those around him to believe in their potential. Ronaldo's style is perfect for those who thrive on energy and excitement. It's about making everyone feel like they're part of something bigger, something special.

These leadership styles have a profound impact on team dynamics. Messi's empathetic approach fosters a culture of excellence and accountability. His gentle guidance encourages teammates to take responsibility for their roles. They know that Messi believes in them, and that belief inspires them to work harder and smarter. His style creates an environment where everyone feels comfortable taking initiative, knowing they have his support. Ronaldo's charismatic leadership, on the other hand, creates a sense of urgency and determination. His assertiveness empowers teammates to step up and lead, to take charge of their own performance. They feel inspired to push their boundaries and achieve the impossible. Ronaldo's approach instills a sense of pride and purpose, driving the team to new heights.

Messi and Ronaldo's leadership has inspired not just their teammates, but young players and fans around the world. Messi's humility and creativity have made him a role model for countless aspiring players. They see him as a beacon of what it means to play with heart and integrity. His leadership shows them that you can be great without being loud, that you can make a difference with kindness and understanding. Young players watch Messi and learn that true greatness comes from within. Ronaldo's tenacity and drive have influenced aspiring leaders everywhere. His relentless pursuit of excellence shows them that hard work pays off. They see Ronaldo as an example of what it means to never give up, to always strive for more. His leadership teaches them that confidence and determination can move mountains. Young athletes look up to Ronaldo and learn that with the right mindset, anything is possible.

Developing a personal leadership style is about recognizing and leveraging your unique traits. It's about understanding your strengths and using them to inspire others. If you're empathetic like Messi, focus on building strong connections. Show your teammates that you care about them as people, not just players. Use your understanding to guide and support them. If you're charismatic like Ronaldo, use your energy to motivate and excite your team. Set high standards and challenge them to rise to the occasion. Encourage them to take risks and embrace their potential. Remember, leadership isn't about copying someone else. It's about finding what works for you and using it to make a positive impact.

Adapting your leadership approach to suit your team's needs is important. Every team is different, and what works for one may not work for another. Be flexible and open to change. Listen to your teammates and understand what they need from you. Sometimes they'll need a gentle nudge, and other times they'll need a push. Be ready to adjust your style to fit the situation. Leadership is about being adaptable and responsive. It's about knowing when to lead from the front and when to lead from the back. By being aware of your team's needs, you can create an environment where everyone feels supported and inspired.

In the world of soccer, leadership is as crucial as skill. Messi and Ronaldo show us that there are many ways to lead, each with its own strengths. Whether you're leading with empathy or charisma, the key is to be true to yourself. Understand your strengths and use them to inspire those around you. By doing so, you can create a culture of excellence, accountability, and empowerment. So, think about what kind of leader you want to be, and take the steps to make it happen.

Chapter 9:

Challenges and Triumphs

Have you ever had a moment where everything seemed to be going perfectly, and then, bam! Out of nowhere, things take a turn? It's like riding your bike downhill, wind in your hair, and then hitting a bump that sends you flying. Life throws curveballs, especially when you least expect them. For Lionel Messi and Cristiano Ronaldo, those "bumps" came in the form of injuries that tried to knock them off their paths to greatness. But instead of letting these setbacks stop them, they used them to fuel their journeys.

Lionel Messi, often called a magician on the field, has had his share of injuries. Early in his career, he faced several hamstring problems that kept him off the pitch. Imagine being in the middle of a thrilling game, feeling like you can take on the world, and then, suddenly, your body says, "Not today, Messi." It's frustrating, right? But Messi didn't let these injuries define him. He took each one as a challenge. One that he could overcome. His knee injuries were another hurdle. These weren't just minor bruises; they were serious enough to sideline him for weeks. Yet, each time, he returned stronger and more determined.

Cristiano Ronaldo, the powerhouse with a flair for the dramatic, faced his own battles with injuries. Knee surgeries and muscle strains were constant companions, always looming in the background. For someone known for his speed and strength, these injuries were major roadblocks. Imagine training hard, pushing yourself to be the best, and then suddenly being told to sit it out. The frustration and helplessness during recovery can be overwhelming. It's like being benched in the game of life. But

Ronaldo didn't let that stop him. He saw these obstacles as opportunities to get better, to come back with even more fire.

Injuries took a toll not just physically, but emotionally too. For Messi, each setback was a test of his mindset. The fear of not returning to his peak form lurked in the shadows. The confidence that once soared could easily waver. It was a battle not just with his body, but with his mind. Ronaldo, with his unstoppable drive, faced similar struggles. Injuries threatened his career momentum, casting doubt on his ability to continue achieving greatness. The emotional weight was heavy. Yet, both players knew they had to fight through, to prove not just to the world, but to themselves, that they could rise above.

The road to recovery was not a walk in the park. It was more like a marathon, requiring patience and persistence. Messi engaged in intensive physical therapy sessions, each one designed to rebuild his strength and agility. These sessions were grueling, but Messi approached them with determination. His training regimens were customized to ensure a gradual and safe return. Ronaldo, with his unwavering dedication, followed a similar path. His rehabilitation involved targeted exercises to strengthen his knees and muscles. He put in the work day in and day out, knowing that each step forward was a step closer to regaining his form.

Their determination and patience in overcoming these setbacks were nothing short of inspiring. Messi's return to the field was a testament to his resilience. After lengthy absences, he didn't just come back; he came back with a vengeance. His performances reminded everyone why he was one of the best. Ronaldo's comeback stories were equally impressive. Stronger and more determined than ever, he showed that no injury could keep him down for long. His return wasn't just about playing; it was about dominating the game with the same intensity and passion as before.

Reflection Section: Your Own Road to Recovery

Think about a time when you faced a setback. Maybe it was an injury, or perhaps a challenge at school. How did you handle it? Write down three things you learned from that experience. Consider how you can apply those lessons the next time life throws you a curveball. Remember, just like Messi and Ronaldo, you have the strength to overcome any obstacle. Keep that fire burning, and never give up.

Battling Adversity: From Doubt to Confidence

Imagine the pressure of having the entire world watching your every move. Now, add the weight of constant criticism. That's life for Messi and Ronaldo. Even when they were at their best, there were always those who doubted them. Messi, who dazzled at the club level, faced harsh critiques about his international performances with Argentina. It's like being the star player in your local league but struggling when you play for the school team. People questioned his ability to lead Argentina to victory, and every missed chance was a headline. For Ronaldo, moving between different leagues brought its own set of challenges. Doubters said he wouldn't adapt, that he wouldn't shine outside his comfort zone. It's the same feeling you get when you move to a new school and wonder if you'll fit in or make friends.

These criticisms and doubts can really mess with your head. Imagine feeling like you have to prove yourself over and over again. Messi faced periods of self-doubt, wondering if he could ever fulfill the expectations placed on him. Each loss with Argentina felt like a weight on his shoulders. He had to reevaluate his goals and ambitions, asking himself what truly mattered. Ronaldo, with his larger-than-life persona, also had moments of introspection. He questioned his choices and wondered if he could continue to dominate in unfamiliar territory. These moments of doubt forced them both to look inward and find new ways to reignite their confidence.

Instead of letting the negativity pull them down, both players found ways to flip the script. Messi chose to focus on personal growth and honing his skills. He knew that if he wanted to silence the critics, he had to become even better. So, he worked tirelessly, fine-tuning his game, and proving that he could lead Argentina to glory. Ronaldo, on the other hand, used criticism as fuel. Each doubter became a reason to push harder. He thrived on proving people wrong, showing that he could excel anywhere. Their ability to transform doubt into determination is a testament to their mental strength.

Triumphs over adversity only made them stronger. Messi's victory with Argentina in the Copa America was a defining moment. It was as if a long-held weight had been lifted. The joy on his face as he held the trophy said it all. He had finally silenced the naysayers, proving that he could lead his country to victory. Ronaldo, too, had his share of record-breaking performances. Each goal in a new league was a statement, a reminder that he was still one of the best in the world. These successes bolstered their confidence, reminding them of what they were capable of.

Messi and Ronaldo's stories remind us that everyone faces doubt and criticism. It's how you respond that makes all the difference. Whether it's on the field or in life, the key is to use those challenges as stepping stones. Find your inner strength, focus on what you can control, and never let anyone tell you what you can or cannot achieve. Just like Messi and Ronaldo, you have the power to turn doubt into confidence and prove that greatness is within reach.

9.3 The Comeback Story: Defying the Odds

Imagine standing on the world stage with the weight of a country's hopes resting on your shoulders. That's where Lionel Messi found himself, facing setback after setback in international tournaments. Critics were loud, and the pressure was immense. But Messi, being the fighter he is, didn't let this define him. He decided it was time for a comeback. The world watched as he led Argentina with renewed vigor. He scored pivotal goals in crucial matches, each one a testament to his determination. Every goal was a message: "I'm not done yet." Messi's resurgence was not just about skill; it was about heart. He reminded the world why he was one of the greatest, turning the doubters into believers.

Meanwhile, Cristiano Ronaldo's story took a different path. After years away, he made a triumphant return to Manchester United. The club where he first became a star welcomed him back with open arms. Fans were ecstatic, anticipating the magic he would bring. But returning wasn't just about nostalgia. Ronaldo knew he had to prove himself all over again. And boy, did he deliver. In crucial fixtures, his leadership was evident. He became the go-to guy, the one who could change the game with a single touch. His presence on the field was electric, inspiring his teammates to rise to the occasion. Ronaldo's return wasn't just a comeback; it was a statement.

Several factors contributed to these incredible comebacks. First and foremost was the unwavering support from their teams and management. Messi had coaches and teammates who believed in him, who knew that with the right encouragement, he could rise again. Their faith acted like a safety net, catching him whenever doubts crept in. For Ronaldo, the support from Manchester United was invaluable. The club gave him the platform to shine, ensuring he had everything needed to succeed. The fans' love and support were like fuel, driving him to reach new heights.

But it wasn't just about external support. Both Messi and Ronaldo had a personal resolve that was unbreakable. They made strategic adjustments to their games, fine-tuning their skills and mindset. Messi focused on what he did best, while Ronaldo adapted his playstyle to fit the team's needs. Their ability to evolve and adapt was key. They knew that to succeed, they had to be flexible, ready to change and grow. This adaptability allowed them to come back stronger, proving that they were not just players but icons.

Key moments marked their return to form. For Messi, it was the goals he scored in decisive matches. Each one wasn't just a point on the scoreboard; it was a symbol of his resurgence. They were moments that left fans in awe, reminding everyone of his unparalleled talent. Ronaldo's leadership in crucial fixtures was equally impactful. His ability to rally the team, to inspire and lead, was evident. He turned challenging situations into opportunities, showing why he was a leader both on and off the field.

The impact of these comebacks on their legacies is profound. Messi reinforced his status as a soccer icon, showing that even the greatest can face setbacks and still rise. His story became one of hope and inspiration, a reminder that perseverance pays off. For Ronaldo, his return solidified his influence in the soccer world. He proved that with determination, you can return to your roots and still achieve greatness. Their comebacks inspired fans and aspiring athletes worldwide. They showed that no matter how tough things get, with grit and determination, you can defy the odds and emerge victorious.

Triumph Over Trials: Inspiring Resilience

Life off the field can feel like a tricky puzzle, throwing unexpected challenges that even the strongest athletes can't dodge. Messi and Ronaldo, despite their fame and skills, have faced their fair share of personal hurdles. Think about family issues that pop up out of nowhere, like a surprise test on a Monday morning. These problems can weigh heavily on anyone, even soccer legends. Messi, with his quiet demeanor, had to navigate the pressures of balancing a demanding career with family responsibilities. It's not always easy being away from loved ones for long stretches. Ronaldo, known for his larger-than-life persona, has dealt with intense scrutiny. The tabloids seem to love him, often trying to pry into his personal life. These off-field pressures are like an unwanted spotlight that never dims.

Beyond family and personal challenges, changes within their teams also test their resilience. Imagine being in a group project at school, and suddenly half your teammates change. New dynamics, new strategies, and the pressure to keep performing at your best can be overwhelming. Messi experienced this when Barcelona underwent management changes. New coaches brought new tactics, and adapting to these shifts required patience and focus. Ronaldo, meanwhile, transitioned between clubs and leagues, each with its own style and expectations. These transitions were not just about adjusting to new styles of play but also about understanding new teammates. Both players needed to find their rhythm quickly to continue excelling.

Amidst all this chaos, Messi and Ronaldo learned invaluable lessons in resilience. They figured out how to keep their eyes on the ball, even when everything around them seemed to be spinning. Maintaining focus in the face of external noise is a skill that requires practice. It's like studying for an exam when everyone else is at a party—tuning out the distractions and zeroing in on what matters. They also developed strategies to manage stress and pressure. Messi, with his calm approach, relied on meditation and visualization to stay grounded. Ronaldo, on the other hand, used intense training sessions to channel his energy and clear his mind.

Their ability to adapt and thrive amidst these challenges speaks volumes about their determination. Messi showed immense leadership during team transitions at Barcelona. He became the anchor, guiding younger players, and ensuring the team stayed united. His quiet confidence inspired those around him, proving that leadership isn't always about being the loudest in the room. Ronaldo's consistent performance, despite changing circumstances, is a testament to his adaptability. Whether playing in Spain, Italy, or England, he delivered outstanding performances. He embraced each new challenge as an opportunity to grow, always pushing himself to be better. His relentless pursuit of excellence inspired teammates and fans alike.

For young readers, the stories of Messi and Ronaldo offer valuable lessons in resilience. Life will throw curveballs, whether it's a tough day at practice or a disagreement with friends. But learning to persevere and adapt is key. It's about finding that inner strength to keep going, even when things get tough. Developing resilience is like building a muscle; the more you practice, the stronger it gets. Another important lesson is taking a proactive approach to challenges. Instead of waiting for things to get better, take action. Find solutions, seek help if needed, and stay positive. Remember, each challenge is an opportunity to learn and grow.

Messi and Ronaldo's experiences remind us that resilience is not just about bouncing back; it's about moving forward with purpose. Their ability to rise above personal and professional challenges is what sets them apart. It's not just their skills on the field that make them legends; it's their unwavering spirit and determination. They show us that with grit and perseverance, we can overcome any obstacle. As you face your own trials, remember that you have the power to inspire resilience in yourself and those around you.

Chapter 10:

BONUS SECTION (Facts and Trivia):

20 Fun & Inspirational Facts About Lionel Messi

1. **The Little Boy Who Grew Big:** As a kid, Messi was diagnosed with a growth hormone disorder, but he never let it stop him. FC Barcelona paid for his treatment, and he grew into one of the greatest players ever!

2. **Messi's First Goal for Barcelona (2005):** At just 17 years old, Messi scored his first goal for Barcelona after a clever assist from Ronaldinho. It was a beautiful chip over the goalkeeper!

3. **The Youngest to Score a Hat-Trick in El Clásico (2007):** At only 19, Messi scored three goals in a single game against Real Madrid, announcing himself as a future superstar!

4. **The "Goal of the Century" (2007):** Messi dribbled past six players and scored an incredible goal against Getafe, reminding everyone of Diego Maradona's legendary World Cup goal.

5. **Breaking Barcelona's All-Time Goal Record (2012):** Messi became Barcelona's highest scorer ever, surpassing the great César Rodríguez. And he kept scoring for many more years!

6. **91 Goals in One Year (2012):** Messi broke a world record by scoring **91 goals** in a single calendar year, more than any player in history!

7. **Four Ballon d'Ors in a Row (2009-2012):** He won the award for the world's best player four years in a row, proving his dominance.

8. **Magical Free-Kicks:** Messi is famous for curling free-kicks past goalkeepers like a magician! He has scored over **60 free-kick goals** in his career.

9. **Olympic Gold Medalist (2008):** Messi led Argentina to a **gold medal** at the Beijing Olympics, showing he was a champion from a young age.

10. **The 2015 Champions League Masterclass:** Messi destroyed Bayern Munich's defense in 2015, famously making Jerome Boateng fall before chipping the ball over Manuel Neuer.

11. **700+ Career Goals:** Messi has scored over 700 goals for club and country, an incredible number that proves his greatness.

12. **The Only Player to Win Six European Golden Shoes:** Messi has won the Golden Shoe award **six times** for scoring the most league goals in Europe!

13. **The "Walking Genius":** Messi doesn't run all the time—he walks, scans the field, and then makes his move like a chess master.

14. **The Copa América Redemption (2021):** After years of heartbreak, Messi finally won **Copa América** with Argentina, proving he never gave up on his dream.

15. **The World Cup Fairy Tale (2022):** Messi won the **FIFA World Cup** with Argentina, scoring twice in the final and finally lifting the trophy he always dreamed of.

16. **Most Goals for Argentina:** Messi is Argentina's **top goal scorer**, even more than Maradona and Batistuta!

17. **The "MSN" Trio:** With Neymar and Suárez, Messi formed one of the deadliest attacking trios ever at Barcelona, winning the **treble** in 2015.

18. **5 Champions League Titles:** Messi has won the **UEFA Champions League** five times, proving he shines on the biggest stage.

19. **The Greatest Playmaker Too:** Messi is not just a goal-scorer; he's one of the best passers in history, assisting teammates like an artist painting a masterpiece.

20. **A Humble Hero:** Despite being one of the greatest ever, Messi remains humble, kind, and a role model for young players worldwide.

20 Fun & Inspirational Facts About Cristiano Ronaldo

1. **A Boy from Madeira:** Ronaldo grew up on the small island of Madeira, Portugal. His family didn't have much money, but he had big dreams!

2. **Hard Work Beats Talent:** Ronaldo was so dedicated that he trained with weights on his feet as a kid to improve his speed!

3. **Sporting Lisbon's Teenage Star:** At just **16 years old**, Ronaldo impressed everyone at Sporting Lisbon with his incredible dribbling skills.

4. **Manchester United's Magic Debut (2003):** Sir Alex Ferguson signed Ronaldo for Manchester United, and in his very first game, he amazed the crowd with dazzling skills.

5. **First Hat-Trick for Manchester United (2008):** Ronaldo scored his first-ever hat-trick against Newcastle, proving he was ready to be a superstar.

6. **First Ballon d'Or (2008):** Ronaldo won his first Ballon d'Or at Manchester United after leading them to a **Premier League and Champions League** double.

7. **CR7's Famous Free-Kick vs. Portsmouth (2008):** Ronaldo's knuckleball free-kick was so powerful that the goalkeeper didn't even move!

8. **Real Madrid's Record Signing (2009):** Ronaldo moved to Real Madrid for a world-record fee, wearing the legendary number 7 shirt.

9. **Fastest Player to 100 Goals for Real Madrid:** It took Ronaldo only **105 games** to reach 100 goals, the fastest in the club's history.

10. **The Bicycle Kick Goal (2018):** Ronaldo scored a **jaw-dropping bicycle kick** against Juventus in the Champions League, and even the opposing fans gave him a standing ovation!

11. **The UCL King:** Ronaldo has won **5 Champions League titles** and is the competition's all-time leading scorer.

12. **Most International Goals Ever:** Ronaldo has scored more international goals than any player in history, proving he's a legend for Portugal.

13. **The Euro 2016 Triumph:** Ronaldo led Portugal to their first-ever **European Championship** title, even coaching from the sidelines after an injury in the final.

14. **Hat-Trick Hero vs. Spain (2018):** In the 2018 World Cup, Ronaldo scored an **epic hat-trick** against Spain, including a last-minute free-kick!

15. **The Juventus Challenge (2018):** Ronaldo moved to **Juventus** and won two Serie A titles, proving he could shine in any league.

16. **A Goal Machine Everywhere:** Ronaldo has scored over **800 goals**, making him one of the highest goal-scorers in history.

17. **A Record-Breaking Return to Manchester United (2021):** Ronaldo rejoined Manchester United and scored twice on his debut, proving he was still unstoppable.

18. **The CR7 Celebration:** Ronaldo's iconic "Siuuuu" celebration is famous worldwide, and kids everywhere try to copy it!

19. **A Fitness Freak:** Ronaldo is known for his insane training routine—he has less body fat than most athletes and can jump as high as an NBA player!

20. **Never Give Up:** Even at nearly 40 years old, Ronaldo is still playing, scoring, and proving that hard work and dedication never go out of style.

BONUS SECTION: TEST YOUR TRIVIA KNOWLEDGE

Ultimate Messi & Ronaldo Trivia Challenge!

Messi Questions (1-25)

1. What country was Lionel Messi born in?

    a. Spain

    b. Argentina

    c. Portugal

    d. Brazil

2. Which club did Messi make his professional debut with?

    a. PSG

    b. Real Madrid

    c. Barcelona

    d. Newell's Old Boys

3. What was Messi's first jersey number at Barcelona?

    a. 19

    b. 30

    c. 10

    d. 7

4. In which year did Messi win his first Ballon d'Or?

    a. 2007

    b. 2008

    c. 2009

    d. 2010

5. How many goals did Messi score in the record-breaking 2012 calendar year?

    a. 73

    b. 91

    c. 85

    d. 100

6. What is Messi's signature dribbling style?

    a. Stepovers

    b. Power dribbling

    c. Close control and quick changes of direction

    d. Rainbow flicks

7. Which club did Messi join after leaving Barcelona in 2021?

    a. Manchester City

    b. Inter Miami

    c. PSG

    d. Juventus

8. What major international tournament did Messi win with Argentina in 2021?

    a. Copa América

    b. UEFA Euro

    c. FIFA World Cup

    d. Confederations Cup

9. How many Champions League titles has Messi won?

    a. 3

    b. 4

    c. 5

    d. 6

10. What is Messi's nickname?

    a. The Machine

    b. The Magician

    c. La Pulga (The Flea)

    d. El Pistolero

11. What was Messi's first senior international tournament?

    a. 2006 World Cup

    b. 2007 Copa América

    c. 2005 U-20 World Cup

    d. 2008 Olympics

12. Against which team did Messi score his first World Cup goal?

    a. Germany

    b. Serbia & Montenegro

    c. Brazil

    d. France

13. How many goals did Messi score in the 2022 World Cup final?

    a. 1

    b. 2

    c. 3

    d. None

14. Who did Messi assist for the game-winning goal in the 2022 World Cup final?

    a. Lautaro Martínez

    b. Paulo Dybala

    c. Enzo Fernández

    d. Ángel Di María

15. What unique record does Messi hold in El Clásico history?

    a. Most goals scored

    b. Most red cards

    c. Most assists

    d. Youngest scorer in history

16. Messi won his first Champions League title in which year?

    a. 2006

    b. 2009

    c. 2011

    d. 2015

17. What is Messi's highest-scoring season in club football?

    a. 50 goals

    b. 60 goals

    c. 73 goals

    d. 91 goals

18. Which club did Messi score his famous solo goal against in the 2007 Copa del Rey?

    a. Real Madrid

    b. Atletico Madrid

    c. Getafe

    d. Sevilla

19. Messi has played for how many clubs professionally?

    a. 2

    b. 3

    c. 4

    d. 5

20. How many Golden Shoes has Messi won?

    a. 4

    b. 5

    c. 6

    d. 7

21. Who was Messi's childhood idol?

    a. Maradona

    b. Ronaldinho

    c. Batistuta

    d. Riquelme

22. How many goals did Messi score in his first Barcelona hat-trick?

    a. 2

    b. 3

c. 4

d. 5

23. Which club did Messi score his first Champions League goal against?

    a. Chelsea

    b. AC Milan

    c. Panathinaikos

    d. Juventus

24. How old was Messi when he won his first Ballon d'Or?

    a. 19

    b. 21

    c. 22

    d. 24

25. What is Messi's preferred foot?

    a. Left

    b. Right

    c. Both equally

    d. None

Cristiano Ronaldo Trivia (26-50)

Early Life & Career Beginnings

26. Where was Cristiano Ronaldo born?

    a. Lisbon

    b. Madeira

    c. Porto

    d. Algarve

27. What was the name of Ronaldo's first professional club?

    a. Porto

    b. Benfica

    c. Sporting Lisbon

    d. Braga

28. At what age did Ronaldo move to Manchester United?

    a. 16

    b. 17

    c. 18

    d. 19

29. What was Ronaldo's first jersey number at Manchester United?

    a. 9

    b. 7

    c. 10

    d. 17

30. Which legendary coach signed Ronaldo for Manchester United?

    a. José Mourinho

    b. Pep Guardiola

    c. Sir Alex Ferguson

    d. Arsène Wenger

Rise to Stardom

31. In what year did Ronaldo win his first Ballon d'Or?

    a. 2006

    b. 2007

    c. 2008

    d. 2009

32. Against which team did Ronaldo score his **first Manchester United hat-trick?**

    a. Chelsea

    b. Arsenal

    c. Newcastle United

    d. Liverpool

33. What is the name of Ronaldo's **famous free-kick technique?**

    a. The Power Drive

    b. The Rocket Kick

    c. The Knuckleball

    d. The Swirl Shot

34. How many goals did Ronaldo score in his final season at Manchester United before leaving for Real Madrid?

    a. 26

    b. 31

    c. 38

    d. 42

35. In which year did Ronaldo transfer to **Real Madrid?**

    a. 2007

b. 2008

c. 2009

d. 2010

Real Madrid Era

36. What jersey number did Ronaldo wear when he first joined Real Madrid?

   a. 7

   b. 9

   c. 11

   d. 17

37. Against which team did Ronaldo score his famous **bicycle kick** goal in the Champions League?

   a. Juventus

   b. Bayern Munich

   c. Barcelona

   d. Manchester City

38. How many Champions League titles did Ronaldo win with Real Madrid?

   a. 3

   b. 4

c. 5

d. 6

39. In what year did Ronaldo score a **record-breaking 17 goals in a single Champions League season?**

   a. 2012

   b. 2014

   c. 2016

   d. 2018

40. What was Ronaldo's **highest goal tally in a single La Liga season?**

   a. 40

   b. 46

   c. 50

   d. 61

Portugal & International Career

41. In which tournament did Ronaldo win his first **major international trophy** with Portugal?

   a. FIFA World Cup

   b. UEFA Euro 2016

   c. Copa América

d. Nations League

42. How many goals did Ronaldo score in **his hat-trick against Spain** in the 2018 World Cup?

    a. 2

    b. 3

    c. 4

    d. 5

43. What did Ronaldo famously do after getting injured in the **Euro 2016 final**?

    a. Left the stadium

    b. Became Portugal's sideline coach

    c. Played through the injury

    d. Substituted himself back in

44. Against which country did Ronaldo score **his 100th international goal**?

    a. France

    b. Brazil

    c. Sweden

    d. Germany

45. How many FIFA World Cups has Ronaldo played in?

   a. 3

   b. 4

   c. 5

   d. 6

Later Club Career & Personal Achievements

46. In which year did Ronaldo leave **Real Madrid** to join **Juventus**?

   a. 2016

   b. 2017

   c. 2018

   d. 2019

47. How many league titles did Ronaldo win with Juventus?

   a. 1

   b. 2

   c. 3

   d. 4

48. What is Ronaldo's famous **goal celebration called**?

   a. The Knee Slide

b. The Tornado

c. The Siiuuu

d. The CR7 Jump

49. How many professional career goals has Ronaldo scored (club + international)?

   a. 500+

   b. 700+

   c. 800+

   d. 1000+

50. What record did Ronaldo set at the **2022 FIFA World Cup**?

   a. Most goals in a World Cup

   b. First player to score in five different World Cups

   c. Most assists in a World Cup

Answers:

1. b) Argentina

2. c) Barcelona

3. b) 30

4. c) 2009

5. b) 91

6. c) Close control and quick changes of direction

7. c) PSG

8. a) Copa América

9. c) 5

10. c) La Pulga (The Flea)

11. c) 2005 U-20 World Cup

12. b) Serbia & Montenegro

13. b) 2

14. d) Ángel Di María

15. a) Most goals scored

16. a) 2006

17. d) 91 goals

18. c) Getafe

19. b) 3

20. d) 7

21. a) Maradona

22. b) 3

23. c) Panathinaikos

24. c) 22

25. a) Left

Answer Key

26. **b)** Madeira

27. **c)** Sporting Lisbon

28. **c)** 18

29. **b)** 7

30. **c)** Sir Alex Ferguson

31. **c)** 2008

32. **c)** Newcastle United

33. **c)** The Knuckleball

34. **b)** 31

35. **c)** 2009

36. **b)** 9

37. **a)** Juventus

38. **c)** 5

39. **b)** 2014

40. **d)** 61

41. **b)** UEFA Euro 2016

42. **b)** 3

43. **b)** Became Portugal's sideline coach

44. **c)** Sweden

45. **c)** 5

46. **c)** 2018

47. **b)** 2

48. **c)** The Siiuuu

49. **c)** 800+

50. **b)** First player to score in five different World Cups

Conclusion

Wow, what a journey it's been! We've explored the incredible stories of Lionel Messi and Cristiano Ronaldo, two soccer legends who have captured the hearts of fans around the world. From their humble beginnings to their rise to stardom, we've seen how these extraordinary athletes have overcome challenges and achieved greatness through their unwavering dedication and passion for the game.

Throughout this book, we've discovered the key ingredients that have made Messi and Ronaldo the soccer superstars they are today. We've learned about the power of mental toughness, the importance of perseverance in the face of obstacles, and the value of teamwork and leadership both on and off the field. These themes have been a constant in their lives, shaping them into the incredible role models they have become.

As we've followed their journeys, we've picked up some essential lessons along the way. We've seen how perseverance, discipline, humility, and adaptability have been crucial to their success. Messi and Ronaldo have shown us that no matter where you come from or what challenges you face, you have the power to achieve your dreams if you stay focused and never give up.

So, what does this mean for you? Well, it's time to take a page out of Messi and Ronaldo's playbook and start setting your own goals. Dream big, just like they did! Whether you want to become a soccer star, ace your exams, or make a difference in your community, you have the power to make it happen. Take a moment to think about what you want to achieve and write it down. Remember, every journey starts with a single step.

As you embark on your own path to greatness, don't forget the lessons you've learned from Messi and Ronaldo. Be a leader, both on and off the field. Show your teammates what it means to work hard and never give up. Be humble in victory and gracious in defeat. And most importantly, always believe in yourself. You have the power to inspire others, just like Messi and Ronaldo have inspired millions of fans around the world.

So, what are you waiting for? Get out there and start chasing your dreams! Remember, greatness isn't just for soccer superstars. It's for anyone who is willing to put in the work and never give up. You have the power to achieve amazing things, just like Messi and Ronaldo. Believe in yourself, stay focused, and never forget that with hard work and determination, anything is possible.

As we come to the end of this book, I want to leave you with a final thought. Messi and Ronaldo's stories are proof that no matter where you come from or what obstacles you face, you have the power to achieve greatness. Their journeys are a testament to the incredible things that can happen when you dare to dream big and never give up. So, go out there and make your own mark on the world. Be the best version of yourself, and never forget that you have the power to make a difference.

Thank you for joining me on this incredible journey through the lives of Lionel Messi and Cristiano Ronaldo. I hope their stories have inspired you as much as they have inspired me. Remember, the world is waiting for you to leave your mark. So, go out there and show everyone what you're made of. I believe in you, and I know that you have the power to achieve greatness, just like Messi and Ronaldo.

References

5 Essential Dribbling Drills for Youth Soccer Teams - Anytime Soccer Training. (n.d.). Anytime Soccer Training. https://anytime-soccer.com/dribbling-drills-for-young-soccer-players-boost-confidence-control-and-creativity/

Abrahams, D. (2018, May 10). *The Powerful Mental Techniques Ronaldo Uses*. LinkedIn. https://www.linkedin.com/pulse/powerful-mental-techniques-ronaldo-uses-dan-abrahams

Arab, A. (2024, June 26). *Cristiano Ronaldo: A Journey of Relentless Dedication and Unwavering Ambition - A Role Model of Hard Work, Sacrifice, and Generosity*. Linkedin.com. https://www.linkedin.com/pulse/cristiano-ronaldo-journey-relentless-dedication-unwavering-arkam-arab-l8cnf

Beano Quiz Team. (2024, August 19). *Ultimate Soccer Quiz Questions For Kids!* Beano; Beano. https://www.beano.com/quiz/sport/ultimate-soccer-quiz-questions-for-kids

Bhattacharyya, P. (2023, September 9). *The Impact of Cristiano Ronaldo and Lionel Messi on Global Football*. Medium. https://medium.com/@bhattacharyyapushan2/the-impact-of-cristiano-ronaldo-and-lionel-messi-on-global-football-b0905afd0c8

Bonn, K. (2024, July 19). *Lionel Messi injury history: Full list of injuries for Inter Miami star from Barcelona, PSG, Argentina*. The Sporting News. https://www.sportingnews.com/us/soccer/news/lionel-messi-injury-history-inter-miami-barcelona-psg/15567b96bcafb5276bf055dc

Brand, G. (2016, January 1). *Cristiano Ronaldo says criticism is part of his success*. Sky Sports. https://www.skysports.com/football/news/11835/10116392/cristiano-ronaldo-criticism-of-my-character

Clarke, D. (2025). *Shoot Like Cristiano Ronaldo: Tips for Precision and Power*. Cupello.Hub. https://my.cupello.com/coaching/advice/shoot-cristiano-ronaldo-tips-precision-and-power

Cohn, P. (2012, October 9). *Staying Confident Against High-Level Competitors*. Soccer Psychology Tips. https://www.soccerpsychologytips.com/2012/messi-and-ronaldo-staying-confident-against-the-best-in-soccer/

Cristiano Ronaldo: Biography, Soccer Player, Al-Nassr Star . (n.d.). https://www.biography.com/athletes/cristiano-ronaldo

Cristiano Ronaldo: From Poverty to Family and Football Superstardom. (2024). SPYSCAPE. https://spyscape.com/article/cristiano-ronaldo-from-poverty-to-family-and-football-superstardom

Dambroz, F., & Teoldo, I. (2023). Better decision-making skills support tactical behaviour and reduce physical wear under physical fatigue in soccer. *Frontiers in Physiology, 14*, 1116924. https://doi.org/10.3389/fphys.2023.1116924

From Grassroots to Glory: Comparing Messi and Ronaldo's Early Careers. (2024, December 21). Messi vs Ronaldo.app. https://www.messivsronaldo.app/articles/from-grassroots-to-glory-comparing-messi-ronaldo-early-careers/

Gennery, E., & Wilks, M. (2015, December 3). *Messi's childhood struggle: Much more than a few injections*. Goal. https://www.goal.com/en-us/news/messis-childhood-struggle-much-more-than-a-few-injections/blt4309705b7ef00fae

Gerage, A. (2018, December 3). *In Team Sports, Chemistry Matters*. Northwestern McCormick School of Engineering; Northwestern University. https://www.mccormick.northwestern.edu/news/articles/2018/12/in-team-sports-chemistry-matters.html

GiveMeSport. (2020, April 12). *Cristiano Ronaldo vs Lionel Messi: 10 great managers that have answered the debate*. OneFootball. https://onefootball.com/en/news/cristiano-ronaldo-vs-lionel-messi-10-great-managers-that-have-answered-the-debate-38942493

GiveMeSport. (2021, July 31). *Cristiano Ronaldo's UCL comeback vs Atletico is one of football's great revenge stories*. OneFootball. https://onefootball.com/en/news/cristiano-ronaldos-ucl-comeback-vs-atletico-is-one-of-footballs-great-revenge-stories-33470847

Hamre, E. (2020, June 21). *Cristiano Ronaldo's Secrets to Success*. Medium. https://medium.com/skillupped/cristiano-ronaldos-secrets-to-success-53a28b8d616f

Hershkovits, E. (2022, July 22). *Mental toughness in athletes: What is it and how to develop grit.* Red Bull. https://www.redbull.com/us-en/mental-toughness-athletes-grit

IANS. (2022, November 20). *Messi, Ronaldo come together for first-ever joint promotion.* The News Minute. https://www.thenewsminute.com/news/messi-ronaldo-come-together-first-ever-joint-promotion-170140

Jones, Dr. F. (2024, December 22). *Case Study: Cristiano Ronaldo's Global Philanthropy - Making a Worldwide Impact.* Jones Consulting Firm. https://thejonesconsultingfirm.com/case-study-cristiano-ronaldos-global-philanthropy-making-a-worldwide-impact

Khan, K. A. (2025, January 21). *Lionel Messi Net Worth and Legacy: The Story of Football's Greatest Icon.* Resident Magazine. https://resident.com/business-and-finance/2025/01/21/lionel-messi-net-worth-and-legacy-the-story-of-footballs-greatest-icon

Kosta König. (2022, November 15). *"Perfect timing to teach Ronaldo a lesson of humility": Fans hail Messi for his heartfelt interview.* Tribuna.com. https://tribuna.com/en/news/fcbarcelona-2022-11-15-perfect-timing-to-teach-ronaldo-a-lesson-of-humility-fans-hail-messi-for-his-heartfelt-in/

La Masia. (2025, February 28). Wikipedia. https://en.wikipedia.org/wiki/La_Masia

Lionel Messi returns from injury in Barcelona victory. (2014, January 8). CNN.

https://edition.cnn.com/2014/01/08/sport/football/messi-barcelona-return/index.html

Lionel Messi: Scientific Analysis of Extraordinary Football Abilities. (n.d.). VIKING BARCA. https://wheecorea.com/messi-mls-champion/lionel-messi-scientific-analysis-of-extraordinary-football-abilities/

Lopes, G., & Torres, Y. (2023, August 11). *Welcome to "Messitown": How Rosario shaped Inter Miami star.* ESPN.com. https://www.espn.com/soccer/story/_/id/38166457/welcome-messitown-how-rosario-shaped-inter-miami-star

Messi & Ronaldo El Clásico Stats. (n.d.). MessivsRonaldo.app. Retrieved March 3, 2025, from https://www.messivsronaldo.app/club-stats/el-clasico/

Messi & Ronaldo Free Kick Record. (n.d.). MessivsRonaldo.app. Retrieved March 3, 2025, from https://www.messivsronaldo.app/detailed-stats/free-kicks/

Mikkelsen, S., & Schwager-Patel, N. (2023, October 26). *Football: Ballon d'Or - Complete list of winners including Lionel Messi, Cristiano Ronaldo and Alexia Putellas.* Olympics.com; International Olympic Committee. https://www.olympics.com/en/news/ballon-d-or-winners-messi-ronaldo-zidane-complete-list

Miller, J. (2023, July 17). *The Messi Effect: How His Leadership Skills Transcend Futbol (aka Soccer).* LinkedIn. https://www.linkedin.com/pulse/messi-effect-how-his-leadership-skills-transcend-futbol-joshua-miller

Ooredoo. (2014, May 8). *Ooredoo and Leo Messi Boost Programme for Children's Health to Three New Markets.* PR Newswire; Cision PR Newswire. https://www.prnewswire.com/news-releases/ooredoo-and-leo-messi-boost-programme-for-childrens-health-to-three-new-markets-258473211.html

Quatrin, F. (2024, December 15). *Lionel Messi and Cristiano Ronaldo almost played together: Where and why the meeting fell through?* World Soccer Talk. https://worldsoccertalk.com/news/lionel-messi-and-cristiano-ronaldo-almost-played-together-where-and-why-the-meeting-fell-through/

Rogers, M. (2024, July 2). *Bench Ronaldo? Portugal is all-in on its star, even more than ever.* FOX Sports. https://www.foxsports.com/stories/soccer/bench-ronaldo-portugal-all-in-its-star-more-than-ever

Sporting CP Portugal Soccer Academy Camps. (n.d.). IFX International Futbol X-Change. https://ifxsoccer.com/sporting-clube-de-portugal-youth-academy/

Sutton, J. (2024, April 1). *Boosting Mental Toughness in Young Athletes & 20 Strategies.* PositivePsychology.com. https://positivepsychology.com/mental-toughness-for-young-athletes/

thomas karapatsos. (2024, February 28). *10 Inspirational Stories of Soccer Stars Who Overcame Adversity.* Soccer Mastermind. https://soccermastermind.com/10-inspirational-stories-of-soccer-stars-who-overcame-adversity/

Voia, M. (2013). *CEP 1301 Youth Training Programs and their Impact on Career and Spell Duration of Professional Soccer Players.*

Academia. https://www.academia.edu/72955224/CEP_1301_Youth_Training_Programs_and_their_Impact_on_Career_and_Spell_Duration_of_Professional_Soccer_Players

What UEFA records does Cristiano Ronaldo hold? (2025, February 5). UEFA.com. https://www.uefa.com/uefachampionsleague/news/0253-0d820b46805f-b78ccae2c451-1000--what-uefa-records-does-cristiano-ronaldo-hold/

www.fcbarcelona.com. (2012, December 22). *Messi ends 2012 with 91 goals*. Www.fcbarcelona.fr. https://www.fcbarcelona.fr/fr/actualites/1146881/messi-ends-2012-with-91-goals

Made in United States
Troutdale, OR
04/14/2025